Praise for *Losing the Cape*

We all want to contribute to something meaningful in thi[s]
Through biblical narrative, fresh writing, and great storytel[ling]
can change the world right where we are.

CAREY NIEUWHOF
Founding Pastor, Connexus Church

This is an important book. In a world obsessed with celebrity, I'm afraid churches have also succumbed. Dan points us back to the truth that God has always deeply used ordinary people, and that ordinary may be one of the most theologically rich words we have.

NANCY ORTBERG
Author of *Looking for God: An Unexpected Journey Through Tattoos, Tofu, and Pronouns*

Poignantly written with a creative ease, Dan Stanford brings to life the realities we wrestle with. Without superpowers available, Dan guides us to where our help comes from, and it's strikingly nearer than we think. *Losing the Cape* will capture your attention and equip you to conquer the villains in your own world.

WAYNE CORDEIRO
New Hope Christian College

Most of us do not see ourselves as any kind of hero. This book by Dan Stanford lifts our sights and stirs us up to believe we actually have the potential to be extraordinary. With personal, endearing examples and the solid support of Scripture, Dan calls every one of us to lean into the power available to us and to soar. A fun and captivating read!

NANCY BEACH
Leadership Coach, Slingshot Group, and author of *An Hour on Sunday* and *Gifted to Lead*

If you're tired of making excuses and ready to start living out your God-given purpose, read this book. Dan Stanford's words will encourage and equip you to be Christ's agent of change in your world. If it's motivation you seek, this book offers a Batman-sized "Pow!"

HEATHER CREEKMORE
Author of *Compared to Who?*

Funny, vulnerable, and wise. Dan offers up a humble and heroic invitation to what it means to be human.

ANDREW BAUMAN
Author of *Stumbling Towards Wholeness: How the Love of God Changes Us*

Do you struggle with insecurity, lack of confidence, and uncertainty that God could use someone like you? If so, this book is for you. And for the record, it's for me too. Dan Stanford's book, *Losing the Cape*, is an engaging page-turner that's full of hope and encouragement that God takes ordinary people and does extraordinary work in and through them.

KEVIN J. NAVARRO
CRM Empowering Leaders and author of *The Complete Worship Leader* and *The Complete Worship Service*

Dan Stanford is a compelling new voice for the church today. *Losing the Cape* can not only re-ignite your heart for God, it can also renew your vision for what God can do through ordinary acts of love, faith, and sacrifice. So what are you waiting for? Read this book, ditch the cape, keep your eyes on Jesus, and go change the world.

Scott Scruggs
Senior Pastor of Northshore Community Church, Kirkland, Washington

As an academic and a lead pastor, I have found that many people are seeking for significance. In *Losing the Cape*, Dan tells us how to find it.

Michael D. Reynolds
Executive Director and Associate Dean, Trinity International University

Each morning, headlines bring tales of real-life villains and threats close at hand. If you're like me, you fear for your security and long for the strength to make a difference in the face of overwhelming odds. Dan Stanford steps in with very good news indeed: you are God's solution to the world's problems, just as you are. No superpowers are needed—only the good gifts that God abundantly provides to mere mortals like us. Dan's deeply personal stories, framed by pain, anxiety, and loss, point toward adventure, justice, and hope. Take courage! All of heaven is cheering you on and victory is assured.

Karen Wright Marsh
Author of *Vintage Saints and Sinners: 25 Christians Who Transformed My Faith*

In this book, Dan demonstrates that the world simply needs more ordinary heroes like us, through whom God can show the greatest power of them all: His extraordinary love for mankind. Dan's sense of humor makes a challenging subject an enjoyable read. May His force be with you!

Maria Metcalfe
Evangelist and author of *Defeating My Goliaths*

Losing the Cape doesn't guilt you into trying to be and do more but rather helps you recognize who you already are. Each page contains truths that explode in your mind with a "Pow!" and a "Bang!" Using humorous stories, biblical insight, and superhero themes, Dan Stanford invites you to stop looking for superhero powers you don't need. You don't need to have a megachurch, a bestselling book, or invitations to the Christian conference speaking circuit. You just need to be you, and you can do it today. Read this book and discover the ordinary hero God created you to be.

J. D. Myers
Author of *Nothing but the Blood of Jesus* and Bible teacher on *The One Verse Podcast*

I don't know about you, but I've always wanted to be an ordinary person who is living an extraordinary life. With creativity, humor, and insight Dan reignites that dream in me! God specializes in using non-superhero types to show that His power works best in available, humble, and surrendered people. This book will inspire you to be all three.

Mike Breaux
Author of *Making Ripples* and *Identity Theft*

LOSING
THE CAPE

THE POWER
OF ORDINARY
IN A WORLD OF
SUPERHEROES

DAN STANFORD

MOODY PUBLISHERS
CHICAGO

All Scripture quotations, unless otherwise indicated, are taken from the Holy Bible, New International Version®, NIV®. Copyright © 1973, 1978, 1984, 2011 by Biblica, Inc.™ Used by permission of Zondervan. All rights reserved worldwide. www.zondervan.com. The "NIV" and "New International Version" are trademarks registered in the United States Patent and Trademark Office by Biblica, Inc.™

Scripture quotations marked ESV are from The Holy Bible, English Standard Version® (ESV®), copyright © 2001 by Crossway, a publishing ministry of Good News Publishers. Used by permission. All rights reserved.

Scripture quotations marked NLT are taken from the Holy Bible, New Living Translation, copyright © 1996, 2004, 2007, 2013, 2015 by Tyndale House Foundation. Used by permission of Tyndale House Publishers, Inc., Carol Stream, Illinois 60188. All rights reserved.

Scripture quotations marked KJV are taken from the King James Version.

Scripture quotations marked NCV are taken from the New Century Version®. Copyright © 2005 by Thomas Nelson. Used by permission. All rights reserved.

All emphasis in Scripture has been added.

Names and details of some stories have been changed to protect the privacy of individuals.

Published in association with The Steve Laube Agency, 24 W. Camelback Rd. A-635, Phoenix, AZ 85013.

Edited by Amanda Cleary Eastep
Interior and cover design:Erik M. Peterson
Cover photo of pulp background copyright © 2013 by WellofMike / iStock (165725810). All rights reserved.
Cover photo of superheroes copyright © 2016 by yogysic / iStock (583859030). All rights reserved.
Author photo: Jeanette Coletta

All websites and phone numbers listed herein are accurate at the time of publication but may change in the future or cease to exist. The listing of website references and resources does not imply publisher endorsement of the site's entire contents. Groups and organizations are listed for informational purposes, and listing does not imply publisher endorsement of their activities.

ISBN: 978-0-8024-1688-9

We hope you enjoy this book from Moody Publishers. Our goal is to provide high-quality, thought-provoking books and products that connect truth to your real needs and challenges. For more information on other books and products written and produced from a biblical perspective, go to www.moodypublishers.com or write to:

Moody Publishers
820 N. LaSalle Boulevard
Chicago, IL 60610

1 3 5 7 9 10 8 6 4 2

Printed in the United States of America

All the great superheroes have a sidekick, a friend with whom they fight crime and share their secrets and struggles. While I'm no superhero, this book is dedicated to three women who make me feel like I can leap a tall building in a single bound. Without their belief in me, this book would never have become a reality.

Suzanne

You put the *her* in hero. Despite the disease that is robbing you of your eyesight, you still see the best in people. You help me defy gravity like Superman even when I feel like a fumbling Clark Kent.

Mom

You were my first sidekick. You were never too busy to throw on a cape and run around the house defeating imaginary villains. Your creativity and optimism helped me believe that saving the day is possible.

Jeanette

Thank you for your friendship. You have a way of helping me believe the impossible can become inevitable.

CONTENTS

HEROES

We might not have Spider-Man's acrobatic flips,
We might not have Batman's "BLAM," "POW" hits,
We might not have Doctor Strange's magic tricks,
We might not even have Superman's gravity defying lift,
We might not have the Flash's lightning fast kicks,
We might not have Wonder Woman's invisible ship,
We might not have Black Canary's sonic piercing lips,
We might not have Professor Xavier's telepathic grip,
But we have God's gifts and a heart to lift
The world out of evil's grip.
We were born for such a time as this;
We are ordinary heroes.

INTRODUCTION

I had a couple of goals while writing this book. Goal number one: don't end up on comedian Jimmy Fallon's late-night talk show segment, "Do Not Read." Goal number two: convince people that as bad as the world is right now, we don't need a superhero to come save the day.

Instead, we need ordinary people like you and me to join God and go change the world right where we are. In the words of nineteenth-century evangelist D. L. Moody, "There are many of us that are willing to do great things for the Lord, but few of us are willing to do little things." It's often the little things that have the greatest impact.

In the animated movie *The Incredibles*, superhero Frozone

and his wife are readying themselves for a night out when he discovers that the city is under attack. He yells to his wife, "Honey, where is my supersuit?" (This line has to be read in the sarcastic voice of Samuel L. Jackson.) Frozone is frantically running through the apartment checking drawers and a secret closet only to find that his suit has been sent to the dry cleaners. When he laments that the city is in danger, she curtly responds, "My evening's in danger."

Do you ever wonder what happened to your supersuit?

You try to subdue your three-year-old through the ancient rite of napping, but she seems to take on superhuman strength as she arches her back and screams like a banshee.

You try to master patience when a Jimmy John's driver is barely doing the speed limit, and you just want to roll down your window and yell, "What happened to *freaky fast?*"

You want to wear your new pair of skinny jeans, but after last night's seconds, they make you look like you've squeezed into the Superman costume you wore when you were six.

Do you ever feel ordinary in a world of superheroes? Do you ever feel like you don't measure up? I hope that by the time you reach the final page of this book, you will feel free to "lose the cape." God didn't send Superman to save the day from a world of brokenness. He sent you.

The structure of this book loosely follows the comic book hero's story arc. Allow me to use two guys named Peter as an example. The first is Peter Parker, better known as Spider-Man.

Most heroes start off feeling ordinary—Spider-Man starts off as a geeky teenager.

An event incites the hero to save the day—Peter is bitten by a radioactive spider, which gives him superpowers. His uncle is then gunned down by a thief (who Peter neglected to apprehend earlier), which is a catalyst to fight for the vulnerable.

Oftentimes the hero struggles with this call—initially, Peter wants to use his incredible powers to make money through pro wrestling.

After a series of circumstances, the hero embraces the call—Peter is challenged by his uncle's dying words: "with great power comes great responsibility."

Along the journey, the hero learns to lean into the help of friends—Peter relies on the support and encouragement of Aunt May and his girlfriend, Mary Jane.

Finally, the hero faces a series of trials as he or she grows into the new identity, while character is built and competence is stretched.

Let's take another Peter as an example. Before Peter was an apostle, he was just Simon. He was a blue-collar fisherman, an everyday kind of guy. Then Jesus calls him to a life of adventure: "Follow me, and I will make you a fisher of men!" (see Matt. 4:19 ESV). He is called to save the day through Jesus' mission, message, and power. Peter is taught to lean into the strength of the community. Jesus sends Peter and the other disciples out in teams of two to bring hope and healing to the world.

Next, Peter struggles with his identity. Like several of the other apostles, Peter is hoping that Jesus is going to crush the Roman overlords and provide the disciples with VIP seats in the kingdom of God. It's only after a series of trials that Peter realizes that Jesus did not come to defeat Rome but to defeat sin and Satan. To be a hero in the kingdom of God will require sacrifice and servanthood. Jesus tells Peter and the rest of His followers something that sounds similar to Uncle Ben's dying words to his nephew. Jesus says, "to whom much was given . . . much will be required" (Luke 12:48 ESV).

I find that our own lives often follow a similar story arc. This book is designed to help you with wherever you are in your story. Chapters 1–4 deal with feeling ordinary in a world of superheroes. Chapters 5–7 explain our call to save the day. Chapters 8–9 promote our need for a team. Chapters 10–18 deal with our struggle with who God has called us to be. Chapters 19–20 deal with two of our tests. And chapter 21 focuses on our embracing the power of legacy.

Ordinary hero, let the adventure begin.

Chapter 1

YOUR NOT-SO-SECRET IDENTITY

My son was only four years old when he asked me if I would pray for him to be miraculously transformed into his favorite superhero (and it wasn't me). We were in the midst of playing superheroes when he called for a time-out. Concerned he might be hurt, I asked him what he wanted me to pray for. With a serious and gravelly voice he whispered, "Pray that God will make me Batman." Instantly I pictured my son as an adult running around in tights, talking like Adam West, and spending a week out of every summer at Comic Con.

Before I prayed, I wanted to know which version of Batman he had in mind. I was willing to pray for just about any version except George Clooney's. My son closed his eyes and folded his hands to indicate that he was serious about his prayer request. He didn't want to just pretend that he had Batman's skills and Bat-suit, he wanted the real thing. He recognized that he didn't currently possess the skills and strength to fight crime and look cool. He wanted to stop dreaming and start being; he wanted an upgrade.

Like my son, we often wish we were a different version of ourselves, a smarter, more successful version. We would love a fatter wallet and a thinner waistline. We want our secret identity to stay secret, mostly because it doesn't fit our idea of a superhero.

I'm not a superhero. When I walk into a room there's no conveniently timed wind blowing through my hair and rippling my cape. For most of my life I struggled to measure up. If life were a Marvel movie, I was an extra who was so unimportant that his name would not be listed in the credits.

As a kid I was always the skinniest one in class. I heard all the insults, like "You're so skinny, you could look through a peephole with both eyes." While I can laugh now, at the time, the only thing smaller than my frame was my self-esteem. Because I was not athletic, I was often picked last or not at all during gym class. I would have taken a hundred dodgeballs to the face just to be picked first for once. I was a C student until college. While the class was noodling problems, I was doodling pictures. I was often lost in a daydream where I was important, powerful, and seen. Partying and drugs eventually became an even more powerful escape.

I would love to say that self-esteem comes with repentance, restoration, and age, but even as an adult, I have continued to struggle with the tension between my potential and my performance. When I married and my wife Suzanne and I exchanged the vows "for better or worse," we didn't realize how much "worse" we would endure. In addition to my wife's physical challenges, the church I started grew more slowly than any of my friends' churches. Although today we hold two services, we are far from the top hundred fastest-growing churches in America.

I have often felt ordinary in a world of superheroes.

I'm willing to bet that I'm not the only one who wrestles with doubts and fears. The reality is that it's hard for us to embrace our present-tense self. We struggle with learning from the past, looking forward to the future, and living in the now. It's so much more tempting to lean toward our future imagined self, the one who gets the awards, has lots of friends, and fits into a pair of skinny jeans.

In 2015, the Bat-suit was one of the most popular costumes for Halloween. My son is not the only one who wants to pretend to have Bruce Wayne's brains, biceps, and billion-dollar resources. In the movie *Batman Begins*, a criminal asks the caped crusader, "Who are you?" After years of wrestling with his identity, finally Bruce Wayne can confidently say, "I'm Batman." Unlike Bruce, it's not always as easy for us to confidently finish the sentence, "I'm _____."

In Exodus 3:11, Moses asks a question all of us wrestle with at some point in our lives: "Who am I . . . ?" God has just asked him to go save the day, and Moses instinctively questions his own identity and competency. When Moses looks in the mirror, all he sees is a shepherd. When God looks at Moses, he sees a servant leader. When Moses reflects on his life, all he sees is an eighty-year-old man whose best days are behind him. God, on the other hand, sees a man who is about to have the most influential forty years of his life. When Moses looks at his insecurities, he sees a man who is afraid of public speaking. God sees a man who will deliver the iconic Ten Commandments and write the first five books of the world's bestselling book, the Bible. Moses sees a life of shearing sheep. God sees a heroic life of saving others. Moses sees the mundane. God sees the miraculous. Moses could have perfect eyesight, but he has terrible insight. He doesn't see himself the way God does.

The way Moses looks at his life reminds me of the Magic Eye pictures that became popular in the '90s. When you first look at a Magic Eye picture, it appears to be a relatively boring pattern of shapes and colors. But when you look at the picture just right—which involves crossing your eyes and looking ridiculous to the people around you—a 3D image appears. Moses sees the boring pattern; God sees the 3D image. Moses is challenged to align his sense of identity with how God views him, to see himself through his heavenly Father's eyes.

When the prince of Egypt was younger, he attempted to stop an Egyptian bully from abusing an Israelite. In his misguided attempt at carrying out his brand of justice, Moses killed the slave driver. Moses, the man who would eventually carve the words "You shall not murder" into stone tablets, had blood on his hands. He was forced to escape before facing trial, leaving the Israelite he had tried to defend just as enslaved as he had always been. It was an epic failure.

For the next forty years, Moses hid in the desert. He gave up on the idea of being a hero. His intentions were good, but he didn't have the strength to back up his heart. But then he heard God say something the Israelites had prayed for: "I have indeed seen the misery of my people. . . . I have come down to rescue them" (Ex. 3:7–8).

After four hundred years of seeing His people enslaved, God is getting ready to flex His muscles. Moses is fired up. He can't wait to hear about God's plan. God has had four centuries to work on it.

Moses, I want you to take your shepherd stick and stand up to Pharaoh and his soul crushing army.

Moses looks at his resume and realizes he's grossly unqualified. *That's your plan? You've had four hundred years, and You come up with an eighty-year-old man and a stick for the solution? Who am I to go toe-to-toe with the world's most powerful nation?*

"Who am *I*?" That's a question many of us wrestle with. Who am *I* to apply for that job? Who am *I* to volunteer at church? Who am *I* to marry someone clearly out of my league? Who am *I* to think I'll ever make a difference in the world?

God never answers Moses's question, but simply says, "I will be with you." God gently reminds Moses—and us—that it's not about our skills and strengths. It's not about our power; it's about God's presence.

How do you see yourself? Do you only see your human failings? Or do you also see the person "being transformed into his image" (2 Cor. 3:18) and equipped "with everything good for doing his will" (Heb. 13:21)?

> *It's not about our power; it's about God's presence.*

We need to realize who we truly are in Christ—we are not weak and powerless. We can have strength, wisdom, courage, and peace. We might not be able to leap tall buildings in a single bound or run faster than a speeding bullet, but we can live in the real power of Jesus' resurrection. And we have purpose.

There are two obvious things that separate us from most of the animal kingdom: opposable thumbs (which is great for text messaging) and self-reflection. Birds never sit around questioning their purpose. Instinctively they just fly, build nests, and chirp outside your window at inconvenient times of the day. The mayfly doesn't buzz around questioning why it only gets twenty-four hours of life while the giant tortoise lives nearly two hundred years. On the other hand, people wonder, wrestle, and worry about who they are.

We tend to define ourselves by the titles we collect, such as son, daughter, husband, wife, parent, grandparent, student, employee, boss, barista, or shepherd. At other times our identity is shaped by our successes and failures: employee of the month, valedictorian, prom king or queen, convict, loser, or alcoholic. We allow ourselves to be identified by our sexuality, ethnicity, gender, and even our favorite sports team.

Humanity's oldest and sometimes greatest exploration is not toward the stars or into the sea, but into oneself. Philosophers challenged their students with the two-word phrase, "Know thyself." We want to know what our purpose is. We want to know if anyone will remember us when we die. We want to know that the world will be a better place because we were born. We want to know that we are contributing as much as we are consuming. The apostle Paul wrote to the Philippian community, "I thank my God every time I remember you." Wouldn't we love to have the kind of reputation that causes others to celebrate when they hear our name?

Every year fifteen million Americans experience identity theft.[1] Millions more give away their identity every day because they believe lies about themselves. They fall victim to the "terrible twos," which are two-word phrases that paralyze us, such as:

I can't.
I'm ugly.
I'm stupid.
I'm poor.
I'm old.
I'm nobody.

We need more truth and fewer terrible twos. We need to be defined by what God says so we can defy the world's stereotypes. Listen to the way King David described himself: "I praise you because I am fearfully and wonderfully made; your works are wonderful, I know that full well" (Ps. 139:14). When is the last time you had a mini worship service to celebrate the way God designed you, your gifts, talents, experiences, and education? We are often better at complaining about who we are and what we can't do than celebrating the richness of who God made us to be.

We lose sight of the fact that we are not just human beings; we are human becomings. Because our character, personality, and skills are fluid, there will always be a gap between our potential and reality. There will always be tension between who we are and who we want to be. We must learn to be comfortable living in the gap: striving, yet content; pressing, yet at rest.

We need to be defined by what God says so we can defy the world's stereotypes.

Perhaps this is what Peter is hinting at when he says, "grow in the grace and knowledge of our Lord and Savior Jesus Christ" (2 Peter 3:18). Grace is not just for our salvation; it's also for our transformation. Grace says that you can love who you are today. Yet it is often so hard to embrace the present tense self and to believe that God could possibly use the present tense, imperfect me.

I had a close friend and roommate who died from complications with type 2 diabetes. Barry provided me with a place to stay when I first became a youth pastor and liked my preaching. Until then, the only compliment I had received was that I had a good reading voice; those are not the words you want to hear as a young preacher, even if you still read off the sermon notes without ever making eye contact.

His funeral is probably one of the most crowded memorial services I have ever attended. People came out not only to grieve his death but to celebrate his life. Our hearts were heavy but our memories were full of light and laughter. While Barry wasn't granted a lot of days on this earth, he made sure every day was a gift. He made the most of his thirty-six years. He liked fast cars, faster motorcycles, and cheesy church jokes like, "Repaint and thin no more." But what he liked more than anything was to make people smile.

Barry never saw himself as someone special. He was often sick because of his erratic blood sugar. Unlike the Israelites who got forty years of manna before enjoying milk and honey, he got the opposite. After a few years of milk and honey he was stuck with manna. He was limited to very bland food—sugar was his nemesis, dessert equaled death. I remember one night when he substituted candy for insulin, and I watched as his body violently shook. In spite of the crippling side effects of his diabetes, like fatigue, dizzy spells, and foggy vision, he refused to stop doing good.

He seemed like an unlikely candidate to save the day, but I know at least fifteen people who owe him their lives. It all started with a small act of kindness. Barry knew a young couple who needed help painting their house, so he volunteered. He owned a painting business and could easily have charged by the hour, but instead Barry saw it as an opportunity to serve. The family he was helping didn't attend church, and he didn't know which way they leaned when it came to God. Barry invited them to one of our church services, and since he had donated so much time painting, they figured they could donate at least one hour listening to a preacher (even though they probably assumed sermons were like dog years—one hour would feel like seven).

To their surprise, this family fell in love with the church and Jesus. The wife then invited her sister, who in turn invited several friends from high school, and they in turn invited friends. Barry's one act of painting led to over fifteen new people entering into the kingdom of God. We should never underestimate these small acts of kindness. The world is changed for the better through them: a kind word, a few moments of time, an invitation.

While the world saw my friend as a frail diabetic whose name will be forgotten within a generation or two, God saw a humble hero. His death didn't grab national or international attention, but his life made an impact on many people who can trace their eternal destinies back to him.

A man named Gideon wrestled with the same question as Moses. God challenged him to go and save the day as well. The future hero effectively asked God, "Who am I?" Listen to his self-defeating words: "How can I save Israel? My clan is the weakest in Manasseh, and I am the least in my family" (Judg. 6:15). Gideon couldn't imagine saving Israel because he couldn't see past his weakness. He was defining his potential by his family's reputation. He saw his current address and family tree as the ceiling to his hopes and dreams. But listen to how God described Gideon: "The LORD is with you, mighty warrior" (Judg. 6:12). Before he stepped foot into the ring, God had already crowned him the champion. Gideon saw weakness; God saw a mighty warrior. Whose opinion would Gideon listen to? Whose opinion will we listen to? Will we allow our own fears and insecurities to hijack our life? Or will we allow God's perspective to shape us?

Superman struggled with his identity until he discovered the Fortress of Solitude. All his life he had felt like an outcast. He couldn't understand why he was so different from everyone else. He was desperate to just be normal. It wasn't until he was able to talk to his father Jor-El (fun fact: El is one of the Hebrew words for God) that his unique gifts make sense. Like Superman, we need to hear from our heavenly Father. Identity should be less about anthropology and more about theology. The one who designed us needs to be the one who defines us. When you stop allowing haters to define who you are and what you can do, you discover that you have more potential to save the day than you realize. You "can do all this" through Christ who gives you strength (Phil. 4:13). You are a gift from God to this world. You have been given talents, abilities, and resources to make this planet a better place. Out of all the genetic possibilities, God chose you. You were born because God knew the world needed you.

You will encounter several "ordinary" people in this book who are making a difference in their corner of the world. They didn't set out to impress anyone, but through small acts of heroism, they have blessed a few. They are not always

> *The one who designed us needs to be the one who defines us.*

recognized or rewarded. Their stories may not be prominent enough to make the nightly news, but you can be certain they have God's attention. We are surrounded by heroes who will never have a billion-dollar movie made about their life. I'm talking about people like:

The college student swamped by homework, yet he helps at the homeless shelter every Tuesday.

The dad who suffers from panic attacks and social anxiety, yet he takes his kids to the theme park, more concerned about their fun than his fear.

The grandmother who is on a fixed income, yet sets aside a little money every month to help support a missionary in a third-world country.

The single mom who hates both of her jobs, yet she shows up every day so she can support her kids.

These individuals don't wear capes, and they don't have a catchphrase like "up, up and away," but they make this world a more beautiful place.

I believe you also have the potential to be one of these ordinary heroes. Like Gideon, you may wrestle with anxiety and inadequacy. You may feel as shaky as an Iron Man bobblehead on the dash of the Batmobile. But God says you are more than how you feel. You are a hero, because the Lord is with you like a mighty warrior (Jer. 20:11). While Moses began with the question, "Who am I?" by the end of his life he could confidently say, "I am the servant of the Lord." God wants you to become confident in your identity in Him as well.

You don't need to wait for a burning bush or a voice from heaven. Your birth was your invitation to go out and change the world, and God is waiting for you to join the cause! You are an answer to someone's prayer. You are God's solution to the world's great needs.

I learned a lot while working on this book. I didn't know that in the original comics, Superman couldn't fly.[2] He was able to leap tall buildings in a single bound, but he couldn't soar through the clouds. I didn't realize that Bruce Banner could only change into the Incredible Hulk at night during the first few issues. His Hulk smash had nothing to do with anger management initially. All his best friend had to do to protect citizens and insurance premiums was lock Bruce Banner (and at one point named Bob Banner) in a room before the sun went down.[3] I didn't understand that Batman used a gun in the first couple of comics. Before trading in bullets for Batarangs, Batman had no problem putting villains in the graveyard rather than Arkham Asylum. Later in his career he had no problem scaring and scarring people, but he refused to shoot. In his view, guns were the weapon of the enemy.[4]

As much as I learned about comic book superheroes, I'm less concerned with the Marvel and DC universe than

I am with our universe. You don't have to suffer from Bat-mania or be a fan of the Man of Steel in order to benefit from this book. You just need to be tired of watching the world implode. Is there something within you that wants to go from passively watching the news to wanting to make the news better? It's not ridiculous to think that you can change the world.

Chapter 2

WHEN THE ORDINARY RISE

Have you ever wished that you could have a superpower? I'm not just talking about the mom stare, the glance that makes a kid go from acting like a fool to keeping his cool. I'm also talking about the ability to turn invisible when you embarrass yourself. Or read minds when you just can't understand what your spouse is thinking.

I would gladly let a radioactive spider bite me if it meant I would instantly have superpowers, like Spider-Man. As a pastor, husband, and father of three boys ranging from toddler to teenager, I can use all the help I can get. Mind reading would be fantastic when trying to pick out the perfect gift for my wife when she's been hinting at something, and I'm just not getting it.

The superpower of predicting the future would have been a game changer on my thirtieth birthday. My family and I were hit head-on by a drunk driver. One moment we were singing happy birthday at a pizza restaurant and the next I was gasping for breath because of the impact. My wife, two young kids, and I were traveling down a dark road toward the condo we where we were staying during a family vacation to celebrate my turning thirty. We were laughing and talking about daddy's pizza party when a car swerved into our lane at full speed. There was no time to brake or react. The cars became one, with a sickening crunch. We all lurched forward, bruising ribs and faces.

It's one of those events you wish could be wiped clean like an Etch A Sketch, but it still haunts me. One scene flashes through my mind more than any other. It's the moment I scooped up my oldest son, blood dripping from his lips and tears streaming down his cheeks. He was only five years old, and he looked at me crying and said, "I just wanted a good life."

Have you ever said that? My son was barely old enough for kindergarten, and he had already learned one of life's most painful lessons. No matter how hard we try to pursue and protect the good life, accidents happen. Sometimes those accidents are caused by a drunk driver committing his fourth DUI. We could have enjoyed one more slice of pizza and missed out on that traumatic experience if I could have peered a few minutes into the future.

As a dad, I try to shield my kids from all of life's dangers. I put safety locks on the cabinets. I read all the ingredients on food packaging to prevent allergic reactions. I check my kids' breathing while they sleep at night. I examine their seat belts before we pull out of the driveway. No matter how many contingency plans I run through, reality reminds me I'm not Superman. I wish I had the Man of Steel's powers so I could shield my kids from all of life's hardships and heartaches, but I don't, and I need help. And while I don't possess the gift of mind reading, I'm pretty confident you would love a little help as well.

> *No matter how many contingency plans I run through, reality reminds me I'm not Superman.*

Globally we are facing racism, terrorism, hunger, war, climate change, and political tension to an exhausting degree. Some mornings you may feel like you've been hit in the face by the Incredible Hulk. Prior to the Industrial Age, people typically only worried about their village or neighborhood. The only thoughts keeping them awake at night were the concerns of their friends, family, and neighbors. Because of the expansive reach of media and the internet, we now know about each natural disaster, every political tension, and any terrorist attack happening around the world in real time. We are consciously aware of not only our own community, but we feel the weight of life in cultures and continents we will never step foot on. It's no wonder the number one drug in

America is anxiety medication. We are virtually omniscient without being omnipotent. Even if we had the combined powers of the Justice League, the global needs seem too great.

Do you ever feel paralyzed by the sheer volume of problems the world is facing? It doesn't help that Jesus refuses to Photoshop life. He's not like the graphic artist who erases blemishes from celebrities and adds six-pack abs. Or the artist who erased a cigarette from a picture of Walt Disney to protect his image.[1] Jesus is honest about life when He says, "In this world you will have trouble" (John 16:33). We would love to have Superman's strength, Iron Man's resources, Professor Xavier's intelligence, and Wonder Woman's immune system and flawless skin, but we don't. It would be great if Christianity gave us superpowers that made us stronger than the world's problems, but instead we often live vicariously through these godlike heroes.

You can't turn on the TV, go to the movies, or surf the web without running into someone from the Marvel or DC universe. From 1938 and the birth of Superman to the present, comic book heroes have not only leapt tall buildings in a single bound, they have skyrocketed to a billion-dollar business. Whether you're a man or woman, boy or girl, a self-proclaimed geek or one of the popular kids, grew up in the burbs or on the street, you have been influenced by the superhero culture. Many of us at some point have tied a sheet around our neck and used it as a cape. I've even been known to put a pair of underwear on my head and call myself Under Dan. I eventually outgrew that (mainly because my wife said it wasn't that cute).

I can't walk through my house without bumping into a superhero. I have three boys who would prefer to live in the Bat Cave. I've invested a depressing amount of money in the superhero franchise. I can't tell you how many Lego superheroes I've stepped on. Wonder Woman, Superman, and the Incredible Hulk have all caused me to recite Colossians 3:8 in the middle of the night, "You must also rid yourselves of all such things as these: anger, rage, malice, slander, and filthy language from your lips." As evidence of how bad it's become, my two-year-old has learned his colors as Hulk green, Iron Man red, and Captain America blue. I sometimes worry that we are going to run out of heroes before he learns all his colors.

It's not just my house that has been saturated by superhero culture. Four out of five broadcast networks currently have some sort of comic book–based TV series. There are twenty-four superhero movies scheduled for 2018 alone. The highest paid actor in Hollywood is Robert Downey Jr., thanks to his lead role in *Iron Man*.[2] Marvel's *Avengers* is the seventh highest grossing movie of all time.[3] The second-highest grossing movie for a female director to date is *Wonder Woman*.[4] And 130,000 people who have the right to vote and make other adult decisions travel to San Diego's Comic Con every July.[5] Grown adults dressed as Spider-Man and Black Widow travel from all around the world to get their super geek on. (As a sidenote, spandex is not for every body type.) Cultural historian Bradford Wright reasons that we have become a comic book nation.[6]

The question I find myself wrestling with is this: why is

it that men running around in tights fighting super villains with ridiculous names like the Penguin, one of the least scary animals, have captured our imaginations and incomes?

In Michael E. Uslan's memoir, *The Boy Who Loved Batman*, Uslan writes that he collected over 30,000 comics before graduating high school because they were "the protective secret sanctum Bat Cave where [he] could escape from the real world and find friends, heroes, and damsels-in-distress who didn't make fun of a boy who read comic books."[7]

Uslan loved his comic book heroes so much that he is largely responsible for getting a grittier Batman to the big screen in the 1989 Michael Keaton version of the caped crusader. I remember standing in one the largest lines I had ever been in to see that movie. This version was a huge leap forward from the campy 1960s Batman in which actor Cesar Romero refused to shave his mustache and instead unconvincingly covered it with white makeup for his role as the Joker.

Clearly Uslan is not the only one who shares humanity's deep need for a savior-figure and turns to superheroes as a valid means of escapism or, maybe more so, an expression of hope. The idea for Superman emerged shortly after the father of co-creator Jerry Siegel died of a heart attack after his barber shop was robbed in the middle of the night. "Many historians believe that this traumatic loss heavily inspired Siegel's bulletproof costumed crusader."[8]

The reality is that we live in a scary world. We tuck our kids in bed at night and try to convince them that monsters are not real. Yet we know that we are surrounded by villains. They may not wear clown masks and have a tragic backstory, but they are just as ominous. They don't hide under beds and in closets, but they jump out when we least expect them. We live in a world where terrorists use women and children as suicide bombers. Although statistics vary widely, the Global Slavery Index estimates that there are more than 45.8 million people in some form of slavery.[9] Bill Federer, an advocate for human rights, claims that there are more slaves now than at any other time in human history.[10]

Loved ones battle cancer, kids go missing. And to compound all these global threats, often the scariest villain lurking in the shadows is ourselves.

We lay awake at night wishing we could aim something like a Bat-Signal toward the midnight sky and know that a hero would appear to save the day. We want the power to control our environment and protect the ones we love. We hate feeling insecure and insignificant. We want a force field around us and all we love. We would love the power to say no to temptation, fix our broken relationships, get out of debt, and heal our hurts.

Our life can often feel as if it has been scripted by the Riddler, that sharp dresser with the green suit who lives to confound Batman. As much as a problem can feel impossible to solve, it can also feel unfair. Why me? Why now? I thought someone was going to come in and save the day, but he never showed up.

A young couple in my church felt that way when they experienced several miscarriages. Every time we got the call that the baby didn't make it, we were all devastated. What made the experience even worse is that this couple was born to be parents. They work in our kids ministry, and the children flock to them. It seemed cruel to be born with a natural desire that kept ending in pain.

During one of my sermons, I shared this quote from Nick Vujicic, a motivational speaker who was born with no arms or legs: "If you have not yet received the miracle you've been praying for, the best thing to do is become a miracle for someone else!"[11] This young wife's immediate reaction was to go get a version of that quote tattooed on her shoulder, and as a couple, they decided to work toward becoming foster parents of kids with special needs. They are choosing to be a miracle for others. They would love to have the power to heal her womb, but they will accept a new mission to heal their corner of the world.

We are desperate for power. We don't want to be weak. But we often feel like Batman after he has been defeated by Bane. In the movie *The Dark Knight Rises*, the muscle-bound villain breaks Bruce Wayne's back and shatters his confidence. After being decisively beaten in hand-to-hand combat, Bruce is thrown into an underground prison. There are no guards and no locked doors. The only potential way of escape is a long climb out of a steep pit with huge gaps between ledges.

A TV is left in his cell broadcasting a live feed of the anarchy taking place in Gotham, a city he has sacrificed to protect. He is now helpless to save the ones he loves. For five months, he is forced to watch and wait. If he is going to escape, it won't be as Batman. He has none of his fancy tech gear. He can't access any of his money. He must climb out as Bruce Wayne. As a boy, he had fallen into a well where he was attacked by bats, and his dad climbed down and rescued him. There is no rescue party coming this time. His freedom and Gotham's redemption rest on his climbing out of the pit. As he claws his way to the top, the prisoners begin to chant, "Deshi Basara," which means "he rises" or "rise."[12]

One of the reasons we are obsessed with superheroes is that we struggle with security and significance. We feel helpless, and yet all of heaven chants for you and me to rise. The author of Hebrews calls this invisible crowd a "cloud of witnesses" (Heb. 12:1). People who witness to the fact that climbing is possible. God is faithful. We are able. Can you hear them chanting? Rise above your circumstances, critics, doubts, failures, fears. In every language, they shout:

Rise.

Rise like a child standing up to the playground bully.

Rise like a man who chooses to forgive his racist oppressor.

Rise like an abandoned wife determined to make a new life for her family.

Rise.

As Bruce Wayne discovers, we don't need to be a superhero or have fancy gadgets to rise and make a difference.

Most people have never heard the name Chris Kennedy, but they have heard of the ALS ice bucket challenge he initiated. In the challenge, people are dared via social media to donate a hundred dollars toward finding a cure for ALS or dump a bucket of ice water over their heads. In 2014, the viral sensation raised over 15 million dollars.[13] I was nominated by a high school student at our church. I gladly dumped ice water over my head and nominated three of my friends. While celebrities who participated got a lot of press, millions of ordinary people made that fundraiser a huge success. The chain reaction was electrifying. It demonstrated just how powerful small acts of kindness can be when the masses rise.

While it's easy to fantasize about saving the day with powers like Superman, Spider-Man, or Shazam, the real heroes make a difference by being different. They choose servanthood rather than selfishness. The choose generosity rather than stinginess. They choose hope rather than despair. They show Christ in the midst of crisis. The beautiful thing about being a hero is that it's not discriminatory. Heroes can be any nationality or ethnicity, rich or poor, men or women, young or old.

For example, in 2016, a video of four hundred students singing the worship song "Holy Spirit" to their dying teacher, Ben Ellis, went viral and was seen by over 32 million people.[14] The high school students had skipped school to encourage their beloved teacher but ended up encouraging millions more as they sang, "let us become more aware of your presence" and Ben mouthed the words along with them. Despite Ben's tragic death a few days later, this moment lives on. We never know what the echo effect of our actions will be.

Listen to what some onlookers said about Peter and John, two of the early church's leaders: "When they saw the courage of Peter and John and realized that they were un-schooled, ordinary men, they were astonished and they took note that these men had been with Jesus" (Acts 4:13). Peter and John were ordinary men and yet they rose from obscurity and poverty to unleash a global movement. The word translated as *ordinary* is the Greek word *idiótés*.[15] It sounds like the English word *idiot*. I don't know about you, but I find it encouraging to realize that God can use idiots. Now don't use this as an opportunity to phone a friend or tap a relative on the shoulder.

When we hear the word idiot, we think of someone who continually makes stupid decisions. That's not what is going on in this passage. The word was used for those who had not graduated from rabbinical school. Peter and John had not attended Jerusalem University to receive a doctorate in theology. Yet, the experts were impressed with Peter and John. Even though they didn't go to the most prestigious school, there was something powerful about what they had to say. They had a spiritual swagger. Peter and John didn't wear super suits. They didn't have catchphrases like "Up, up and Yahweh!" or "It's Hallelujah time!" They didn't own a Bat Cave or a Fortress of Solitude. But they changed their world through the power of the Holy Spirit.

> *You don't need an "S" on your chest when you have the Savior in your heart.*

What we need to know is that whether you have a GED or PhD, you can be used by G-O-D. What matters most is not the certificate on the wall but the calling on one's life. You don't need an "S" on your chest when you have the Savior in your heart.

Now I'm not dismissing higher education; I have a master's degree. But I will take the Holy Spirit over higher learning any day: "'Not by might nor by power, but by my Spirit,' says the LORD Almighty" (Zech. 4:6). The disciples were spiritual heroes. Throughout history God has used the ordinary to accomplish great things: He used the young David to stop a giant, He chose Esther to save a nation, and He used a young woman named Mary to bring Jesus into the world.

In the Bible and throughout human history, it has not just been the top 2 percent who have made the world a better place; it is the 98 percent. God has often picked the commoner instead of the celebrity—a teenager who invites the new kid to sit at her table or the pastor with only a dozen people in his church, yet he preaches every Sunday like he is talking to thousands.

Are you ready to become a real-life spiritual hero as well? Are you ready to rise?

Chapter 3

UNDERDOGS OVERCOME

One of the first heroes I ever saw as a kid wasn't a Norse god named Thor, a Kryptonian named Superman, or a spider-bitten teenager named Spider-Man. My first hero walked on four legs, chased his tail, and would have loved kibbles and bits. His name was Underdog. All he had to do was take a power pill, jump in and out of a phone booth, and suddenly he morphed from an unassuming puppy named Shoe Shine into a muscle-bound superdog. He would triumphantly announce, "There's no need to fear! Underdog is here!" As a skinny kid built for sports like checkers and getting beat up, I found Underdog's story inspiring. It gave me hope that I too could become a hero despite being small and shy.

An underdog is defined as "a competitor thought to have little chance of winning a fight or contest."[1] Like many fictional heroes, Underdog proved that the least likely can save the day. He was a reminder that we live in a world where underdogs can overcome: David can beat Goliath, a turtle can beat a rabbit, and the Chicago Cubs can win the World Series after over a hundred years of struggle and loss (and with only a 20 percent chance of winning[2]).

Underdogs are a reminder that victory does not automatically belong to the strong, successful, and statistically favored. Han Solo is a perfect example. In a famous scene from *The Empire Strikes Back*, Solo, the renegade pilot of the Millennium Falcon, is dizzyingly maneuvering the spacecraft through an asteroid field when C-3PO, the droid, says, "Sir, the possibility of successfully navigating an asteroid field is approximately 3,720 to 1!" Solo wisely shoots back, "Never tell me the odds."[3] The classic underdog, Han Solo knows that while statistics can be scary, they never tell the whole story.

When I started a church, people made a point of telling me that 80 percent of church plants fail. When I started writing a book, many people told me that 78 percent of books sell fewer than five hundred copies. The truth is that God defies the odds all the time. When Peter dared to step out of the boat, statistics were not in his favor. When the Israelites marched around Jericho, history would suggest that there was a 100 percent chance their stroll around the city would not work as a battle strategy. But Christian underdogs overcome when they focus on their Savior and not just on stats.

Cancer patients given a terminal diagnosis can defy the odds.

Children born into broken or dysfunctional families can experience restoration.

Former drug addicts can overcome their codependence.

An inexperienced pastor fully reliant on God can create a thriving community.

According to Barna Research, 46 percent of American churchgoers attend a church with fewer than one hundred members.[4] Many congregations will never hit triple digits. In an age of celebrity pastors and congregations large enough to have their own zip code, this can be intimidating. Most of these small-church pastors are never invited to lecture at leadership conferences; they are not featured on *Time*'s list of the top 100 influential people in the world. But the reality is that God has never been limited by size or resources.

> *God has never been limited by size or resources.*

Small churches can be like worker ants, which can lift up to five thousand times their body weight. Only in eternity will we know just how huge an impact the small congregations will have on the world. Impact is not based on the size of the congregation but on the actions of the congregation. When a church of any size exercises faith, hope, and love in their community, they make a kingdom impact. The goal is not to be a megachurch but to have a mega impact no matter the size of your church.

Do you ever feel like an underdog?

Maybe you were just an average student. Maybe you didn't get past the first round during the annual spelling bee. Maybe you felt sick to your stomach just thinking about the teacher calling on you. According to standardized test results, most of us are not intellectual giants. Only around 2 to 5 percent of the population have the IQ of a genius.[5] Now, this doesn't mean the rest of us are dumb, but it might mean we won't be having a conversation about astrophysics or quantum mechanics with Stephen Hawking. Not all of us are called to be the next St. Augustine, Tertullian, or Descartes.

Former President George W. Bush once joked at a commencement speech, "To those of you who are graduating this afternoon with high honors, awards, and distinctions, I say, 'Well done.' And as I like to tell the C students: You too can be president."[6] There are many politicians, pastors, and professionals who were not on the honor roll. Successful leadership has a lot more to do with a person's ID—their character and competence—than their IQ.

When I was in graduate school, grades became my god. I about killed myself striving for straight As. I stayed up late reading encyclopedia-sized books on theology and church history. I carried flashcards everywhere I went. My wife yelled at me one time for memorizing Greek words during a wedding ceremony. I responded sarcastically, "Gynai oupo hekei he hora mou," which is Greek for "Woman, my hour has not yet come." By the way, just because you can quote Jesus in the original language doesn't mean you won't ever have to sleep on the couch.

I am a perfectionist, and I wanted to have top marks on every quiz, test, paper, and presentation. My perfectionist nature is one of the reasons why I refuse to clean windows, because I can never get them perfect. I can always find a stubborn streak. The problem with that is that you only have so much time and energy each day. While I was in graduate school, I was simultaneously leading a church plant and raising three young kids. I should have been satisfied with simply maintaining sanity. But when I got my first B I was super depressed. I wondered how could I ever be a successful leader without straight As. How could I ever preach tweetable sermons with a B on my report card?

I struggled with this. I was embarrassed when I realized I would not graduate at the top of my class. It was hard for me to come to grips with the fact that excellence is not perfection; rather, it is doing the best you can with what you have. The truth is I would not be a more effective pastor or better writer today if I'd gotten straight As. Most people don't ask me what my GPA is before I get up on stage. I was putting undue pressure on myself. But we don't have to be an academic all-star in order to be used by God. Grades don't define us; God does.

Maybe you feel like an underdog because you were never very popular. You were picked last at recess, no one invited you to the prom, you feel left out during work huddles, or you sit alone at church. Did you know that only one in ten thousand people will ever be truly famous?[7] Most of us will never have a video go viral. Most of us will never be known on a national or international level. Most of us will never have a movie made about our life.

Even in the Bible, only a few thousand people are named.[8] That might sound like a lot, but consider the millions of people who lived over thousands of years. We don't know many of the names central to what God did on the planet. We don't know the names of the four friends who brought the paralyzed man to Jesus for healing. There's a guy doing the snoopy dance on the streets of heaven because of those four people, but their names have been lost to the very selective memory of history. We don't know much about the boy who gave his five loaves and two fish to Jesus so that thousands could be miraculously fed. This was the only miracle to be recorded in all four gospels, yet we don't know that boy's name. You can be anonymous on earth and yet famous in heaven. God loves to use the underdogs to accomplish His purposes.

In 2 Corinthians 12:9, the Lord gives a reason for this to the apostle Paul, who pleaded with Him to remove a (unknown to us) thorn from his flesh. The Lord says, "My grace is sufficient for you, for my power is made perfect in weakness." Paul's reaction reveals a lot about how our response and the indwelling of God's power are linked: "Therefore I will boast all the more gladly about my weaknesses, so that Christ's power may rest on me."

Ruth is a classic example of an underdog. Shortly after her story begins, we learn that she had lost her husband and had been through years of famine. She lived at a time when women were seen as second-class citizens and were vulnerable unless they had a husband, father, or son's protection. She had no children and was probably thought to be barren. She was a Moabite woman who had chosen to accompany her Jewish mother-in-law Naomi back to the land of Judah, where Moabites were unwelcome: "No Ammonite or Moabite or any of their descendants may enter the assembly of the LORD, not even in the tenth generation" (Deut. 23:3). It was also an ancient Jewish practice to wipe the dust of a foreign territory off one's feet so as to remove any contamination. And you thought hand sanitizer was extreme! If there was Moabite dust on your sandals, you might as well toss them out and buy a new pair.

Imagine how Ruth must have felt, a refugee in a country where she was looked down upon because of her ethnicity. It would have made more sense for her to abandon Naomi and return to her mother's family. But Ruth was willing to face an uncertain future because of her faithfulness to Naomi. In spite of this sacrifice, I don't think Naomi realized how valuable Ruth truly was. When the two women finally arrive in Bethlehem, everyone was shocked to see Naomi and wondered if it was really her. "'Don't call me Naomi,' she told them. 'Call me Mara, because the Almighty has made my life very bitter. I went away full, but the LORD has brought me back empty. Why call me Naomi? The LORD has afflicted me; the Almighty has brought misfortune upon me'" (Ruth 1:20–21).

Did you hear what Naomi said? I guarantee Ruth did.

But had she really come back empty? Wasn't Ruth standing right next to her? In the moment, all Naomi could see was what she had lost. There's a reason this story is called the book of Ruth and not the book of Naomi. It's through Ruth that Naomi would soon have plenty of food to eat. It's through Ruth and her eventual marriage to Boaz that Naomi would have grandchildren. In fact, by the end of the book it was said that Ruth is better to Naomi than seven sons (see Ruth 4:13–15). What an incredible compliment in a culture where sons were seen as more valuable than daughters. It's significant too that the number seven is used here, since it is the number of completion. Although Ruth was the greatest possible gift, Naomi initially saw her as a burden. But the truth is that often burdens are blessings in disguise.

Naomi couldn't see the whole picture. She was not empty-handed. Naomi returned to her homeland with a greater gift than she could possibly have imagined. In fact, it was through this Moabite woman and Boaz that not only would King David be born, but several generations later, Jesus Himself. Eventually the book of Ruth would be chosen by the Jewish community to read each Pentecost (or Shavuot). Out of the thirty-nine books in the Old Testament, it is the only book named after a non-Jewish person. I'm sure there are other reasons (such as the fact that it speaks to the lineage of Jesus), but I find it significant because Ruth's story is a reminder that God uses underdogs. He frequently uses the most unlikely of people to bring about His purposes. Although there are no overt miracles in the four short chapters of Ruth—no burning bush or parted sea—God was working to orchestrate every detail. History is His-story, and many times God propels His story forward by using underdogs like Ruth.

History is filled with them. In the 500s, a plague swept through Europe that infected many. The pope at the time died from the crippling disease, and the church was without a leader for six months. Unanimously, people voted in a monk named Gregory, but like Moses and Ruth, he didn't feel qualified to lead. While he was born into wealth and was highly educated, when approached about the papacy, he said that he was "so stricken with sorrow that he could scarcely speak." He ran away and hid in the woods. A group of people chased him down and dragged him back to Rome. Personally, I would have loved to hear Gregory's first sermon. The poor guy may have felt like an underdog, but he ended up one of Rome's greatest popes. History would remember him as Pope Gregory the Great.[9]

> *It is the Holy Spirit who will empower you and enable you.*

Some of the best leaders were not the ones who volunteered or felt qualified. Some of them had to be chased down, dragged back, and talked into being a hero.

Esther was too scared to confront the king at first and had to be convinced that she was born "for such a time as this" (Est. 4:14).

Elijah, running for his life and at the end of his rope, prayed for God to take his life (1 Kings 19:4).

Timothy wrestled with anxiety. Paul had to encourage him with the words, "For the Spirit God gave us does not make us timid, but gives us power, love and self-discipline" (2 Tim. 1:7).

It is the Holy Spirit who will empower you and enable you. Your natural talents, impressive IQ, financial portfolio, or caffeinated personality are not the most important qualifications, because God uses the underdog.

Chapter 4

NOT JUST HEROES AND ZEROES

When I proposed to my wife, I gave her a diamond ring. This has become such a tradition that the diamond industry has grown into a $72 billion business. We say, "Diamonds are a girl's best friend," while dogs are man's best friend. That seems fair. We give diamonds to say "I'm sorry," "I love you," and "You're special to me." It's customary for a man to spend around two to three months' wages on a ring.[1]

This may shock you, but Adam did not give Eve a diamond ring. For thousands of years people got married without making a jeweler filthy rich. In fact, the tradition of giving a diamond ring didn't start until 1477, when Archduke

Maximillian of Austria proposed to Mary of Burgundy with a diamond-encrusted ring.[2] Of course a man with a name like Maximillian started this tradition. It wasn't until the 1940s that it became normal for the average Joe to give a diamond ring to his bride-to-be.[3]

While diamonds seem impressive, they are just compressed carbon. They are only valuable because culturally we have said it is so. We have been told that "every kiss begins with Kay." But lots of things are made from carbon, including people, who are 18 percent carbon.[4] Why do I bring this up? Because millions of people buy diamond rings as a way of expressing their love without ever taking a second to pause and wonder, why *do* we give diamonds?

In life, some things are perceived as more valuable than others simply because society has collectively assigned value. We will pay over a hundred dollars for a pair of sneakers because of the symbol on them instead of because they are the best for our feet. We will heed the opinions of celebrities, not because they are the most educated or experienced, but because they are famous. We will cheer for a particular sports team because of the state or family we were born into, not because they hold the best record. We will pick a church because it's where our friends or family go without stopping to ask whether it's spiritually healthy.

Perceived value is not the same thing as intrinsic value. While society might see people as valuable if they are talented, beautiful, intelligent, or famous, human worth has nothing to do with what we do. Rather, it's all about who we belong to. For example, my son has a stuffed animal named Ducky. He has had this cuddly critter since the day he was born. It is faded, missing stuffing, only has one eye, and has been puked on. It originally cost twenty dollars and even though my son owns things that are more expensive, if there were a fire, it is the first thing he would grab, then maybe the dog, and then his brothers. You must have your priorities. The way my son looks at his duck is the same way God looks at us. We are broken and beat up, yet God sees us as invaluable.

> *We are broken and beat up, yet God sees us as invaluable.*

In God's eyes, the world is not made up of heroes and zeroes. God would see Spider-Man and the person who cleans up his spider webs the same way. Spider-Man is a litter bug leaving behind webs and criminals. If you have ever cleaned up Silly String after a birthday party, you know what a big job that is. Now imagine having to go throughout New York City cleaning webs off skyscrapers. (Fans will say that the webs dissolve after a few hours, which still requires cleaning up the residue and criminals left behind.) In this imagined universe, think about the farmers and fast-food workers who must make all the food to fuel the Flash. Running at speeds exceeding the speed of light, he burns through a ridiculous number of calories. As an ectomorph who burns through a thousand calories when he sneezes (don't hate), I know from experience the Flash would need a grocery store's worth of food every day. All that food represents dozens of workers. Or think about the construction workers who must clean up after the Hulk's temper tantrums. His catch-phrase is, "Hulk smash," not "Hulk clean up."

Whether you're a superhero or a behind-the-scenes servant, we have all been made from the same stuff. In Genesis 1:27, Moses records the revolutionary words, the ultimate life hack: "God created mankind in his own image, in the image of God he created them; male and female he created them." We don't know at what point these words would have been shared with Israel, but I can just imagine Moses sitting near the pillar of fire by night sharing these empowering words for the first time. Keep in mind Moses was speaking to people who had been slaves for four hundred years. In Egypt, it was believed that Pharaoh represented God. He was considered to be the image bearer of the Creator.[5] Slaves were at the other end of the spectrum. Moses flips this and says it's not the top 2 percent but rather all of us—men, women, slave, and free—who have been created in God's image. God doesn't make zeroes.

When I started this church, I was told that my influence would be ten years older and ten years younger than myself. That bit of advice sounded wise but proved false. The first married couple I baptized, Barb and Dave, were in their seventies. Both forty years older than I, they revolutionized how I saw the older generation. At the time, our church met in a gymnasium, so everything was transient. We had to arrive a few hours before service to set up all the chairs and equipment. Barb volunteered to make coffee at home and then transport it to the school. In addition to the fresh brew, she would always bake cookies and treats for us. The kids—and a few adults—would wait at the door for Barb to show up. My favorite was her lemon bars, which my kids fondly called "lemon Barbs." In addition to being one of our biggest servers, she also made sure that she gave every week to our Giving Hope fund, which was money that was set aside to help hurting families.

One week, a lady shared with me that she was on her way to church praying about how she could afford a coat for her granddaughter for Christmas. When she arrived, she received a gift card from this ministry without anyone knowing about her prayer. That gift card was made possible because of Barb's generosity. Barb got to be an answer to prayer. Her kindness was another person's miracle. The world needs more Barbs.

"God created mankind in his own image, in the image of God he created them; male and female, he created them" (Gen. 1:27). This verse gives us a dose of humility and dignity. Humility because of what God creates us from. Did you know that the word *Adam* means dirt?[6] God could have created Adam from anything, but He chose dirt. "Then the LORD God formed a man from the dust of the ground and breathed into his nostrils the breath of life, and the man became a living being" (Gen. 2:7). Adam was made from the same stuff that you can find on the bottom of your shoes. Dirt is everywhere. Dirt makes up 10 percent of the planet.[7] It's ridiculously valuable, but we don't treat it that way. We don't buy dirt jewelry.

We say things like "that person said a *dirty* word."

Now the Hebrew word for dust or dirt is simply earth. We know that people are made up of water, oxygen, carbon, hydrogen, nitrogen, and calcium. The point is that God made man from earthly substances, common elements. When I was growing up, my parents put a piece of artwork on my bedroom wall with the following poem: "Girls are made of sugar and spice and everything nice. Boys are made of snips and snails and puppy dog tails."[8] The word *snip* means a small or insignificant person. I think they were unintentionally trying to tell me they wanted a girl. But while humankind is made from dirt, God's breath within us makes us extraordinary. God starts with dirt and creates something worth dying for.

> *Humankind is made from dirt; God's breath within us makes us extraordinary.*

Recently my kids were debating about stage names for their imaginary band. One of them said, "My name is Funk." The other echoed, "My name is Jazz." Collectively they announced, "And together we make *Junk*!" Kids are fun. God does not see you as junk. Your parents may have said you were an accident. The divorce paper may have communicated you were unlovable. The eviction notice may have made you feel like a financial failure. Unemployment may have made you feel worthless. But your value is not based on a majority vote. God loves the alcoholic as much as He loves the missionary. God's love isn't withheld because of our failures or lavished based on our accomplishments. In the words of Max Lucado, "We are human beings not just human doings."

God doesn't measure the value of a human life the same way we do. We use measurements such as net worth, number of trophies, GPA, academic letters attached to a person's name, number of social-media followers. God measures our worth based on the fact that we are His creation and Christ died for us. We are an extension of His heart. All of us can put a smile on His face or a tear in His eye.

In the Sermon on the Mount, Jesus tells us just how precious we are to Him: "Are not five sparrows sold for two pennies? Yet not one of them is forgotten by God. Indeed, the very hairs of your head are all numbered. Don't be afraid; you are worth more than many sparrows" (Luke 12:6–7). To Jesus, the price of one human soul is infinitely greater than the world and all it offers. That includes the price of the Mona Lisa (valued at over $100 million),[9] Bill Gates's house ($123 million),[10] and one of the most expensive diamonds, the Cullinan ($400 million).[11]

You can tell how valuable something is to a person based on what they are willing to pay for it. Jesus loved you so much He was willing to pay with His life to purchase you back from death and the devil. While an insurance company might say that one human life is worth $7.4 million, Jesus would say you are priceless.

Yet we often treat ourselves and others infinitely less valuable than we are. We treat the barista differently than we do our favorite celebrity. We treat the elderly differently than we do a cute little baby.

When God chose to create stars, sunsets, and seagulls, He spoke them into existence. With a thunderous voice, He said, "let there be . . ." and things exploded into being. But like a mom yelling up the stairs for a child to clean his room, speaking worlds into reality can be done from a distance. With Adam it was different. We can surmise God knelt in the mud; Deity getting dirty. He grabs some clay and begins to shape the first of billions like Him. I'm sure God whistled as He shaped the heart that was made to love Him . . . molded the eyes that were designed to look to Him . . . formed the hands that were engineered to express His touch in the world.

But Adam needed one more ingredient before going from molecules to miracle. God bent down, placing His lips against His new creation, and breathed. Oxygen filled the young man's lungs. His heart began to race; his consciousness became alert; and his senses flooded with sounds, smells, and warmth. The first thing Adam saw was the face of God.

Maybe kids teased you when you were growing up. Maybe it doesn't seem like anyone would miss you if you were not around. Maybe you can no longer do the things you did when you were younger. But know this—you are a divine and living work of art.

Most people don't pray for their kids to be average. We don't daydream about living the common life or getting lost in the crowd. We don't go to the theater to watch stories about mediocre heroes named *Couch Potato Man.* "Wow, he can flip through channels at an impressive speed."

Even the disciples were guilty of jockeying for positions of influence. James and John even put their mom up to asking Jesus if they could each sit on the Master's left and right side throughout eternity. It was the equivalent of asking Jesus if they could be second in command. There's something within us that longs to be known. But what A-list celebrities can tell you is that the applause of people is never enough. The paparazzi, autographs, and "selfies" leave you feeling empty. Only the smile of God can truly satisfy. It's the reason why the Jewish priests were instructed to pray this blessing over God's people: "The LORD bless you and keep you; the LORD make his face shine on you and be gracious to you; the LORD turn his face toward you and give you peace" (Num. 6:24–26).

> *While you may be ordinary in the world's eyes, you are extraordinary in the heart of God.*

You are a combination of molecules and miracles. When you realize that you're created in God's image, then you realize that while you may be ordinary in the world's eyes, you are extraordinary in the heart of God. Jesus believes you're worth dying for. The people you lock eyes with every day are also worth saving because they reflect God's image as well. Maybe they are doing a poor job of it, but under all their mess is a masterpiece.

Chapter 5

CREATED FOR ADVENTURE

I am no longer naturally adventurous. I don't daydream about climbing mountains, jumping out of planes, zip-lining through rainforests, or eating anything spicier than a seedless jalapeño. Some days I feel like the antithesis of the dare-deviling superhero. I prefer to keep my adrenaline around the same level as a decaf cup of coffee.

I like my adventures domesticated. I want to experience them from the comforts of a chair, popcorn in one hand and a remote control in the other, watching a comic book movie. I love adventures when it's someone else's life on the line, when the characters are fictional, scripted, and have stunt doubles to do the dangerous stuff. But while I prefer to avoid risk, I feel challenged by God to leave my bubble of perceived safety. I'm convicted by the words God speaks through the prophet Amos, "Woe to you who are complacent in Zion" (Amos 6:1). The Hebrew word translated here as *complacent* means "careless security."[1] Those last two words haunt me. Have I allowed my life to drift toward careless security? While there's nothing wrong with locking the doors, wearing a seat belt, or chewing a few times before swallowing, there is something tragically wrong when safety becomes our idol.

While adventures scare me as an adult, I loved them as a kid. The neighborhood woods were full of dinosaurs, aliens, soldiers, dragons, and wizards. Sticks were swords. Overgrown foliage provided paths yet to be discovered. The world was full of lost treasures, endless possibilities, and untamed hopes and dreams. Punishment as a kid was being stuck inside. Now my kids act like I'm torturing them to send them out into the yard away from their electronic devices. Just because we call it a living room doesn't mean that's the space in which God intended us to live. The world wasn't meant to be explored through a screen; it was meant to be felt through scrapes and bruises as you fall trying something new. As creatures made from the dirt, we have a primal need to get dirty.

Unfortunately, the older we get, the easier it is for us to replace risk for responsibility, purpose for paychecks, and sacrifice for safety. The key is to grow older in wisdom and younger in heart.

St. Francis of Assisi was challenged to leave his life of comfort to follow Christ. He grew up at a time when the

Catholic Church was very rich while a large percentage of the population was poor. The church owned a third of the land in Europe,[2] and they collected 10 percent of people's wages with the threat of excommunication if a person didn't pay. Multimillion dollar cathedrals with vaulted ceilings and elaborate artwork were built right next to houses that looked like Dorothy's house when it first arrived in Oz. In this context, Francis chose to live a voluntary life of poverty to challenge the church's corruption.[3] "Preach always and if you have to, use words" is a phrase often credited to him. This spiritual leader may not have said these words, but he definitely lived them out. He was willing to leave comfort to become a catalyst for change.

I was at a leadership conference listening to a friend of mine talk about the value of risk. He started a church with fifty people, and it grew to over three thousand. Attendance was growing, lives were changing, marriages were being restored, the addicted were finding hope, their building was state of the art, and they had all the financial resources they could possibly need. But then he felt God call him to walk away and become a consultant for struggling churches. As I heard him talk about leaving, I found myself thinking, *How could a person ever walk away from a church they started? That's like walking away from one of your kids. I could never do that!*

Then I felt like God asked me, "Are you open or closed to whatever I want to do in your life? Have you put up no trespassing signs? Have you predetermined what you think I will and will not ask you to do? Are you led by your fears or by your faith?" To become a spiritual hero, God must have

> *We can't save the world if we worship at an altar of safety.*

an all-access pass into our life. He must be free to call us out of our comfort and complacency into the adventure He created us for. We can't save the world if we worship at an altar of safety.

Most fictional superheroes have a touch of DRD4, the so-called "risk-taking" gene. As Iron Man, Tony Stark straps rockets to his hands and feet. Spider-Man swings through New York traffic. Bruce Banner quadruples in size to become the Hulk, risking embarrassment because there is no way his pants are keeping up with that extreme growth spurt. Granted we don't need the DRD4 gene or rockets on our feet, but we will need to operate outside of our comfort zone from time to time.

I had the privilege of helping start a church in Ireland in 1999. The biggest thing standing in my way wasn't money. When the church heard I couldn't afford it, they raised all of my support money in five minutes. I couldn't believe they were that eager to get rid of me. My biggest hurdle was fear.

I hate heights. I don't like any height above six feet, one inch tall, which conveniently is my height. I have a visceral response to high places. I get dizzy, panicky, and feel like I'm falling. I've tried to overcome it all my life, forcing myself to ride roller coasters, go to the top of large buildings, jump off a fifteen-foot-high platform, and even climb to the top of rock walls. Unfortunately, the fear never completely goes away.

My biggest hurdle in going to Ireland was the idea of flying for over seven hours. My fear of heights means I don't like to fly. I've never said like Jimmy Hendrix, "I want to kiss the sky." I've flown several times and I've never found a reason to enjoy it. I hate the turbulence, ear popping, layovers, lost luggage, nauseated stomach, and the screaming kid kicking my seat. I know logically that flying is statistically safer than driving a car.[4] The Wright brothers' invention has an admirable track record. But my emotions scream, "What goes up must come down, and planes don't always wait for a landing strip to make their descent." I worry that I'm on the one plane that goes down out of the five million that reach their destination safely.

Because of my irrational fear, I don't even like the song "I'll Fly Away." I hope God just beams me up when I die. One second I'll be reading a good book and the next second I'll be in heaven. I would hate to be the first person to get sick on my way. I picture myself hovering like Jesus and losing my lunch around the stratosphere. That's not what you want to be known for throughout the rest of eternity.

With these irrational thoughts bouncing around my head, I tried to talk my way out of the trip to Ireland, but I couldn't escape the nudge of God. This was something I was supposed to do. As I got on the plane bracing myself for thirty-six thousand feet in the air, I opened a random book I had brought and the bookmark inside read, "If I go up to the heavens, you are there. . . . if I settle on the far side of the sea, even there your hand will guide me" (Ps. 139:8–10). Peace washed over me. When we allow fear to interfere in our life, our world can become too small.

Would you consider yourself adventurous or cautious? Do you take the same route to work every day? Do you compulsively order the same item off the menu? Do you have the same routine at the gym month after month? Do you have the same haircut you had ten years ago?

One of the challenges of living a life of adventure is that it often comes at a price. As humans, we tend to pray for safety and security. We want God to be our bulletproof vest. We surround ourselves with airbags, knee pads, memory-foam pillows, hand sanitizer, and two-ply toilet paper. While we gravitate toward comfort and ease, being a hero can occasionally demand sacrifice. Just as a mother sacrifices her body to give birth to life, so heroes make sacrifices to breathe life back into a dying world. Heroes, at times, must be willing to sacrifice comfort, money, time, reputation, and even relationships.

When Mary was chosen to give birth to Jesus, she had to give up her reputation. Carrying the Savior of the world through divine conception came at the price of people thinking she was either mentally unstable or promiscuous.

Peter and John were asked to leave family and friends, a successful fishing business, and presumably all the hush puppies they could ever want. Despite the cozy life, they were challenged to leave and receive all that God wanted to do in them and through them.

The primary symbol of Christianity is not a Captain America shield, but a cross. While the cross has become art in our culture, in the first century, no one would have dreamed of wearing a cross as jewelry, a tattoo, or decoration around their house. We have sanitized the cross, wiping it clean of blood and pain. When Jesus said, "Whoever wants to be my disciple must deny themselves and take up their cross" (Matt. 16:24), His disciples understood that the adventure of following Him and rescuing others would come at a cost. It's terrible marketing. But what Jesus wants people to know is that following Him will not always be easy. It will not always be convenient and comfortable. Following Jesus is hard to do from the comfort of a chair. But the benefit is immeasurable.

What are you willing to sacrifice to make an eternal impact on this world? We can work so hard to avoid death and discomfort that we miss out on life. There's a scene in the first Captain America movie where Steve Rogers is in boot camp. His superior officer doesn't want him in the military and doesn't believe he will make a very good soldier. He describes Steve as a "ninety-pound asthmatic." To prove Steve and his troop are not worthy and ready for combat, the officer throws a grenade toward the crowd of soldiers. Everyone instinctively runs away but Steve throws himself onto the fake grenade.[5] He's willing to sacrifice his life to save everyone else. That's what heroes do.

When my youngest son was two months old, we discovered he was allergic to milk. My wife had to give up all dairy so that he would stop getting sick after every feeding. That meant she had to give up ice cream for him. The one thing my wife loves more than me is ice cream. I'm confident she would leave me for Ben or Jerry. But she was willing to sacrifice because she loves her son.

In the same way, we may have to sacrifice something we love and have worked hard for to help others. During these moments of sacrifice it's important to remember that God is not a sadomasochist. He doesn't call us to suffer without purpose. Jesus is a great example of this. No one could harm Jesus until the cross. Herod tried to kill Him when He was just a baby. Satan tried to sabotage His mission and ministry in the desert. People tried to throw Him off a cliff after His first sermon. The religious community tried to stone Him to death when He compared Himself with God. Jesus was bulletproof until the cross. God shielded Him until His death would serve a higher purpose. The cross not only represents sacrifice, it also represents hope and healing. It was through the cross that Jesus could rescue people. Only God knows what eternal impact is on the other side of your sacrifice.

I grew up with the adage, "Better safe than sorry." I've even used it with my kids. But is that crippling phrase always true? Don't we often find reward on the other side of risk? God told our ancestors to "be fruitful and increase in number; fill the earth" (Gen. 1:28). Taking a risk or stepping outside of the nice square boxes we live in can be tough, even for an ordinary hero. We like our boxes—four solid walls, clean right angles, little cutout windows to peer through. When you were a kid, what was more exciting than your parents buying a new washing machine? Okay, lots of stuff, but it was all about the giant cardboard box. That thing became your fort, your Fortress of Solitude. You vowed to live in it forever.

It's even harder to step out of a box we've been in for a long time. Abram was ninety-nine when God paid him a visit and made a covenant with him, one that was so big it came with a name change. Abram became Abraham, and he and his wife would finally bear a son together in their old age. Not only that, but God would greatly increase his numbers. "God said to him, 'As for me, this is my covenant with you: You will be the father of many nations . . . I will make you very fruitful; I will make nations of you, and kings will come from you'" (Gen. 17:3–6).

God, like a momma bird, sometimes must push us out of the nest to help us fly. You see, home is not where the heart is; home is where the heart of God is. Are you chasing His heart? I am not naturally adventurous but supernaturally I'm willing. I don't want to miss out on what God wants to do in me and through me by playing it safe.

Isn't it better to risk in an effort to serve and possibly falter than to live a life of safely missing out? Remember that we had to leave the security of our mother's womb in order to enter a dangerous world to experience all that life offers. We should live lives our grandkids will be inspired by. To do this, we must tap back into our childlike thirst for adventure. One of my favorite quotes about adventure comes from the children's book *Winnie the Pooh*. Pooh says to Christopher Robin, "As soon as I saw you I knew an adventure was going to happen."[6]

I wonder if the disciples felt the same way when they heard Jesus' words, "Follow me." Did they anticipate three years of miracles and radical life change? Did they wake up every morning on the edge of their seat just waiting for another leper to be healed, storm to be stilled, dead person to be raised, or religious know-it-all to be put back in their place? Growing up, I felt the invitation to follow Jesus was primarily about escaping hell. That's not the offer Jesus made to His original followers. The offer He made was about engaging life.

> *If Jesus left the comforts of heaven, don't you think He might ask you to leave your comfort zone from time to time as well?*

Jesus went on the greatest adventure to rescue you. He left the comforts of heaven where everyone adored Him. He had no critics; no one wanted Him dead. Angels flew around constantly reminding Him how awesome He is. He left all of that to face the devil and death for you. If He left the comforts of heaven, don't you think He might ask you to leave your comfort zone from time to time as well?

Listen to the conversation between Jesus and Peter in Mark 10. When Peter exclaims, "We have left everything to follow you!" (v. 28), Jesus replies, "Truly I tell you, no one who has left home or brothers or sisters or mother or father or children or fields for me and the gospel will fail to receive a hundred times as much in this present age: homes, brothers, sisters, mothers, children and fields—along with persecutions—and in the age to come eternal life" (vv. 29–30).

I bet Peter wishes Jesus would have left out that phrase, "along with persecutions." I know I do.

That's not the invitation that's offered. The trail Jesus blazes will not be straight or safe. But each step will lead toward growth, opportunity, miracles, meaning, freedom, and peace. Are you following Him?

Chapter 6

THE *HER* IN HERO

M y two oldest boys love to ask me hypothetical questions. For instance: Would you rather be born with an elephant trunk or a giraffe neck? If I say giraffe neck, they will point out all the challenges of having a giraffe neck, like driving a car. If I say I'll drive a convertible so I can stick my head out the top, they will ask me about all the bugs that will get stuck in my teeth. If I concede and say fine, I choose an elephant trunk, then they will point out the challenges of having a trunk for a nose. Imagine how gross it's going to be when you get sick; two-ply tissues won't be strong enough. What are you going to use to blow your nose? At this point I tell them that I'm going to use their bedding and then make them sleep in it. The reason why they like this game is that it creates a no-win situation, and it feeds into their boy humor.

There's a scene in *The Dark Knight Rises* where Batman is faced with an impossible decision: he can either save the woman he loves or the man he believes can save the city. Will he put his heart or Gotham's needs first?[1] Life doesn't always give us an easy option. Sometimes we are handed a challenge that is impossible to change, and we are forced to cope with it.

Superheroes face a lot of local, national, and global challenges. Besides constantly having to save the day, they often have personal challenges to overcome as well. Tony Stark must deal with panic attacks after helping to save the world from an alien invasion.[2] Peter Parker has to deal with the death of his girlfriend when the Green Goblin drops her from a bridge and his alter-ego Spider-Man is only milliseconds from saving her.[3] Bruce Wayne must overcome a dislocated back in order to rescue Gotham from the villain, Bane. In our quest to make the world a better place, we must overcome personal challenges as well.

My wife and I were blindsided by a personal challenge in the winter of 2007. Suzanne was having some trouble driving at night and was plagued by throbbing headaches throughout the day. We scheduled an eye exam thinking that she might need to upgrade her glasses prescription. We joked about what she would look like if they had to give her a pair of bifocals. Suzanne already had hearing loss since birth, so she wondered if the vision problems were connected.

During the exam, it was obvious that the doctor was becoming alarmed. He showed us a picture of a "normal" eye and then showed us a picture of Suzanne's. Without any optometry training we could see that the two pictures were very different. Finally, he said words that redefined our life: "You appear to be going blind." So much for breaking the news to us gently. He stressed that my wife needed further exams to confirm his suspicions, but he was confident in his diagnosis.

We had just had our second child and had recently started a church. We were looking forward to the future. Now we didn't know how much of the future she would be able to see. Sometimes you choose the Mount Everest–sized challenges in life. You pursue the summit of a graduate program; you scale the mountain of starting a new business. At other times, mountains are just dropped in front of you. There is no choice but to climb or cower. The mountain of blindness was not a giant hill we were prepared to face, much less climb.

After a series of tests, we discovered that Suzanne has Usher syndrome type 2, which includes the vision condition retinitis pigmentosa.[4] It's a big word that's hard to spell and even harder to live with. Usher syndrome is a degenerative disease with progressive loss of both hearing and eyesight. My wife is daily being robbed of two out of her five senses.

I did a lot of complaining during those first few months. Why her? Why her eyes and ears? Why couldn't it be her sense of smell? Living with four males, a loss of smell could have been a blessing. Why not a psychopath or pervert instead of a woman who uses her eyes to see the best in people? The condition only affects four out of every one hundred thousand people in the developed world, so why her? Why us?

Was I ready for my wife's "can't do's" to become my "have to's"? She couldn't drive, clean the house, or navigate life as easily as she used to. Was I ready to endure what I call a secondhand handicap? How could I prepare to watch her world grow smaller and smaller? Would I lose my smile as she lost her sight? Would the woman whose blue eyes were one of the first features I fell in love with one day no longer see me? How would this impact our marriage and ministry? We were devastated.

The unknowns are sometimes the most brutal. Suzanne hasn't been able to drive now for ten years. She has no peripheral vision and has no idea how long until the world fades to black. She doesn't know when beautiful sunsets, Broadway shows, and baby smiles will become a mixture of memory and imagination. When we exchanged vows in 2002, we had no idea what "for better or for worse" was going to mean. She gets daily migraines. She no longer has the independence to go where she wants. She stubs her toes on a weekly basis. That alone will bring a person to their knees.

Suzanne has always believed God's grace is sufficient to get us through anything. Being diagnosed with a degenerative condition challenged that perspective when she grasped the likelihood of how it would affect the future too. She knows she may not be able to watch our sons walk down the aisle. She won't be able to recognize the color of their eyes in our grandchildren's faces. In spite of the hurts of losing independence and the uncertainty of what the future will look like—literally—Suzanne chooses to surrender herself to God's grace daily, sometimes hourly, and follow His lead.

When I found out my wife was going blind and deaf, I prayed desperately. As she lost her sight, I lost my voice.

What started as a cry for God to do the impossible became a whisper as I wrestled with the inevitable. I would reluctantly punctuate my prayers with "Thy will be done." But I always assumed God's will would someday align with mine. It was inconceivable for me to think that God would allow her to be robbed of her sight. It made no sense. Being a full-time pastor of a church plant is hard enough without having to navigate all the stresses and challenges that come with disability.

As time went on, I began to resent the story of Jesus healing blind Bartimaeus in Mark 10. As I watched my wife run into objects she couldn't see, I hated the reminder that Jesus could whisper a few words and dead cells and cones would instantly spring back to life. All it would take was a single word from Him, and yet there was only silence. My prayer closet began to feel very lonely. Prayer stopped feeling powerful and effective. A few years ago, I made up a rap that communicated how I felt at the time. It was raw and real.

> I have my face to the floor
> Crying out to the Lord
> I'm in the midst of a war
> and I'm not sure
> I can overcome my doubts
> and all of my fears
> I have too many question marks
> attached to all my tears
> I'm sitting in this pew
> feeling all alone
> they call it God's house

but is He home?
I don't know.

I was preaching, counseling, visiting people in the hospital, serving food at the homeless shelter . . . all the usual tasks, but inside I was dying. Heroes don't always have the luxury of serving from a place of wholeness and tranquility. Sometimes they must cheerlead faith while wrestling with doubt. They must be the light while struggling with darkness. They must bring healing while nursing their own wounds.

My theme verse in life is based on Mark 9:24: "I believe; help my unbelief!" (ESV). While I want to be like Paul, I'm a lot more like Thomas. I often have more question marks than answers. I say my faith is like a thousand-piece puzzle. I have eight hundred of the pieces, but I'm missing two hundred. There are enough pieces to see the picture, but there are holes. And to be honest, they bother me deeply at times.

What I have come to realize is that faith and doubt are not like a light switch. It's not like either you have a 100 percent faith or a 100 percent doubt. Sometimes it's situational. You trust God with your money but not your health or with your health but not your relationships. And when we struggle with our faith, it's hard for us to leave our comfort zone. We need to pray, "I believe; help my unbelief!"

A poem helped me greatly during this season of struggle. The poem, quoted by a chapel speaker, was one of the only lessons I remember from my freshman year of college. "When all around you is darkness, and you don't know what to do, get on your knees and pray, until the light breaks through." During one of those dark nights, I prayed for God to help us if He chose not to heal Suzanne. With the constant change in vision and hearing, she often feels unsure of herself at home when I can't be there. It became clear that we may need to consider getting a service animal. In 2013 we learned about a family who breeds Labradoodles for the purpose of service. Each puppy cost more than two thousand dollars, a bit out of our price range. So we hesitantly prayed. To our surprise, the family heard our story and donated a puppy to us that we named Chloe.

While our new dog didn't come with a price tag, she still needed several supplies. We went to a local pet store and began the shopping spree. As the clerk rang up all the necessities the grand total came to a whopping three hundred dollars. I was thinking, *I don't even spend that much on my kids!* I didn't anticipate our four-legged miracle being so expensive. When I got home, I showed Chloe her new stuff and then checked the mail. To my surprise, there was a random check for the same amount we had just spent.

> *Many times I would hand God suggested revisions for our story, and He would hand me Scripture.*

God has consistently chosen to provide us with what we need to help navigate blindness instead of healing my wife's eyes. Many times I would hand God suggested revisions for our story, and He would hand me Scripture. Verses like 2 Corinthians 12:9: "My grace is sufficient for you." I felt like He said to me, "Suzanne will see things blind that she would not have seen with 20/20 vision because of the lives I touch through her." I have seen that come true over and over as she has been able to bring hope to others in their struggles.

When I was a kid I would hold my hands up to my eyes in the shape of binoculars. I'm sure you have done the same at some point in your life. The intent is to focus your vision and empower you to see further. All it really does is block your peripherals and create tunnel vision. That's how my wife sees these days. She has little to no peripheral vision. She can't see people approach her from the side, which means I unintentionally scare her often. I laugh. She strikes.

Her central vision is missing a few puzzle pieces, which means her eyes are constantly straining to adjust. I tell you this because one of the ways in which she loves to serve is through graphic design. For a few years, she helped out an MS charity by creating all their marketing materials pro bono. She suffered through massive headaches because she believed in the cause. She loved being a part of raising money to empower a person who lost mobility and independence by providing a motorized wheelchair. On another occasion, she painstakingly handcrafted jewelry to help a family raise money to bury their two-year-old who had died tragically.

My wife was classically trained on the piano from the time she was a little girl. One of the things that brought us together as a couple is that I wrote lyrics, and she would compose the music. The last public performance she played was Laura Story's song "Blessings." The lyrics end with this question: "What if trials of this life, the rain, the storms, the hardest nights, are your mercies in disguise?"[5] That was seven years ago, and we are still discovering God's mercies during misery. Blindness is not easy. We don't wake up in the morning singing shouts of praise because of the challenges that come with this journey. But we do lean into God, trusting Him to give us the grace for the day and look for the little ways in which He uses our hurts to bring hope and healing to others.

I recently read *Life Without Limits* by Nick Vujicic to my kids. Nick was born without arms or legs, yet he still surfs, plays soccer, and travels. He is not defined by his handicap, he defies it. His joy and optimism are contagious. Nick keeps a pair of shoes in his closet. They remind him that God still does the impossible. He says, "If you can't get a miracle, become one."[6]

Every morning my wife chooses to be a miracle to someone else. She chooses to defy her disability rather than be defined by it. Her favorite motivational statement is "choose joy." She chooses to celebrate rather than complain. She reaches for the next level when she chooses to lean into faith rather than fear. She looks for ways to invest in others when she has every excuse to be served. She truly puts the *her* in hero.

When life deals you an impossible situation you must make some choices as well. You not only go through pain, you grow through pain. Some of us grow more bitter or jaded. We stop trusting people. We justify giving in to our shadow side. The world owes us. We grow in doubt. God is cruel or He doesn't exist. We grow cold and self-centered. But some of us grow in character and hope. We are determined to help others. We refuse to let tragedy define us.

We use our wounds to heal others. Pain pushes us closer to God and toward fulfilling His mission for our life.

While God did not cause the problem, He can create a cause out of the problem.

The recovering drug addict can become a sponsor.

The victim of rape can help rescue people from human trafficking.

The neglected child can be an awesome parent.

The ex-gang member can use his story to rescue teens from that path.

While God did not cause the problem, He can create a cause out of the problem. Are you choosing to climb the mountains that have fallen into your path, or are you allowing them to stop you from moving forward? Who knows what opportunities are just beyond your mountain or how many lives are waiting for you on the other side? There are lives that need to be inspired by your story.

Chapter 7

PROTECT YOUR CITY

'm not built for fighting. I look like the character from *Where's Waldo* on a diet. Can you imagine getting punched by Waldo? There's a reason why he's hiding all the time. Despite my biceps being the size of a mosquito bite, I've always had a soft spot in my heart for the underdog. I don't like to see people get picked on or bullied. I'm a pacifist by nature. I don't mind Jesus' statement to turn the other cheek, but I refuse to watch injustice if I can do anything about it.

One day when I was a kid, I was sitting toward the back of the bus daydreaming about Little Debbie snacks and what cartoon I was going to watch when I got home. When I looked up, I noticed a kid pummeling my best friend, Cofee (yes, *KO*-fee). Cofee was getting beat like a piñata on Cinco de Mayo. The fight was unfair; the bully hit puberty early and could grow a beard in fifth grade. Instinctively, I jumped on his back and managed to wrestle him off my friend. I was proud of my heroic act until I remembered that this bully and I got off the bus at the same stop, alone. I learned that day that sometimes fighting for the underdog comes with a black eye. Sometimes being the hero hurts. Protesting can mean time in jail; speaking up can mean getting unfriended on social media.

When I turn on the news, I'm tempted to put on a cape, learn parkour, and assume a secret identity like Pastor Dantastic. I can't passively watch the world implode. There's something in the heart of a hero that wants to fight for truth and justice. There are enough tragedies in the world to keep any hero from taking off their mask and returning to their day job. Headlines range from terrorist attacks to marital spats. We have figured out how to put a man on the moon and a super computer in our pockets, but we still haven't eradicated homelessness, poverty, world hunger, racial tension, or abuse. Everyone wants to know who is going to come save the day.

Before we lace up our knee-high superhero boots, we need to admit that only God is big enough to clean up humanity's messes. While we are created in God's image, that does not include His infinite wisdom or omnipotent strength. We cannot eradicate poverty, reverse climate change, or cure cancer on our own. On most days, we are lucky if we can control our own temper, waistline, and wallet. Our strength may seem insufficient when compared to the world's big, hairy, stinky problems, but with God, we can protect the underdogs, even if it may cost us a few bruises.

Our weakness is not an excuse to sit on a couch, watch a Marvel movie, and do nothing. While we are not capable of saving the whole world, we can parallel ourselves with God's plan and make a difference in our corner of it. We have been strategically placed in our neighborhood, among our family, and in our line of work. There are people in our lives that only we can influence and protect.

There's a scene in the Bible where Jesus heals a man plagued by evil spirits. Grateful, the guy wants to go on tour with this miracle worker. He wants to tell everyone how awesome the Son of God is; he wants to be Jesus' walking infomercial. Strategically, Jesus tells him to go back to his friends and family (see Mark 5:18–19). In effect, Jesus is telling him to go back to the people who saw him before he was cured, where he would have the greatest impact. In the same way, God wants to strategically place you where you can have the greatest impact as well. Sometimes that's the school, job, favorite coffeehouse, or neighborhood you are currently in . . . or it's the place He's trying to nudge you toward.

According to recent data, more than 70 percent of American workers don't like their jobs.[1] Most people don't wake up singing TGIM (Thank Goodness It's Monday). Before I was a pastor I was a sanitary engineer, a fancy term for toilet cleaner. I didn't go to college for that role; it's not what I dreamed of as a kid or what showed up under my spiritual gifts test. It was simply the only thing available at the time. The job was brutal, and the company I cleaned for looked down on

> *Sometimes work is less about passion and more about provision.*

janitors as second-class citizens. I daily reminded myself of the years Jesus served as a carpenter. He didn't leave heaven because the world needed a better construction worker. Sometimes being a hero means going to a thankless job and making less than you're worth. Sometimes work is less about passion and more about provision.

I know a single dad whose wife left him for heroin. When his wife left, it was like his life left with her. Despite his world collapsing in on him every day, he dragged himself to work. He swung the hammer and turned the screwdriver even when he was depressed and broken, because two little kids were at home depending on him. He was a hero every time he refused to hit the snooze button and give up on life. He knew he was responsible for protecting his family no matter what it cost.

We all have our own city to protect, like most comic book superheroes. Superman protects Metropolis. The Caped Crusader is always a Bat-Signal away from coming to Gotham's rescue. The Flash is a lightning-fast shield around Central City. The Black Panther is a warrior-king fighting for Wakanda's protection. Several comic book cities have a hero whose sole focus is on its protection.

I find it interesting that there are a lot of superheroes who are responsible for New York, including Spider-Man, the Watchmen, Dare Devil, and the Punisher. Obviously, New York needs a lot of help. One person said that living in New York is like living in Stephen King's head. Granted, this is an exaggeration. Cities, like rural areas, are a combination of beauty and brokenness. Cities tend to be the backdrop for superheroes because the concentration of people amplifies the rate of crimes. I imagine if the Statue of Liberty could talk, she would have some heart-wrenching stories to tell.

There are thousands of cities in the United States, from Los Angeles to New York. My church plant is located between Milwaukee to the north and Chicago to the south. Cities are deceptive. When you fly into a city, the skyscrapers, museums, and parks are gorgeous from thirty thousand feet in the air. Cities do attract creative and ingenious dreamers who come to the city to make their mark on the world. But most cities are a combination of beauty and tears.

When you go off the beaten path and explore the back alleys, you also find gangs fighting over city blocks, rampant homelessness, children with few resources and fewer opportunities, men and women on street corners forced to do unspeakable things, and people strung out on drugs . . . all of this within blocks of billion-dollar buildings. This brokenness is but a hint of the darkness that can be seen in every pocket of the globe. I find it interesting that God's vision for humanity began in a garden. In the garden of Eden, there was no need for police officers, pastors, or paramedics. If I were to sum up the heartbeat of God in one word, it would be *shalom*. The Hebrew word for peace, shalom means harmony between God, man, and nature. There was no need for super-heroes in the garden. There were no dark alleys that you had to avoid. There were no funerals, divorce papers, or anxiety medications. There were no tragic stories for news channels to report. This was life as it was meant to be. This was the life Adam and Eve were called to protect.

The life that we so desperately fight for and elusively chase was lost by our ancestors in two short chapters. We barely get past the opening credits before the story spins out of control. Adam and Eve failed to protect the garden they had been blessed with. They inherit an entire planet and an all-access pass to God, but they wanted the one thing God said was off limits. It would be like me taking my son to an ice cream shop and offering him any flavor except for peanut butter because he's allergic to nuts.

Now imagine he insists on peanut butter because he feels like I'm withholding something good from him. He can trust my good intentions and enjoy chocolate chip or butter-scotch ribbon, or he can jump over the counter and shove a bite of peanut butter ice cream down his throat, then suffer from hives, stomach pain, and shortness of breath. Adam and Eve rob themselves and others by trying to gain more. Like so many of us, they ruin everything with their blind hunger and lack of trust. They don't realize that God's moral fences are God's defenses. God's direction is our protection. We can fall into the same trap.

You're married but you find yourself on the internet late at night looking for someone else.

You have dozens of shoes but you max out your credit card to buy just one more pair.

You are diabetic and the doctor keeps telling you to avoid sweets, so you promise to quit after just one more bite.

Adam and Eve failed to obey God and properly enjoy and steward the garden God had provided. Listen to Satan's crafty sales pitch: "God knows that when you eat from it your eyes will be opened, and you will be like God, knowing good and evil" (Gen. 3:5). Satan implies that God is holding back, and they deserve more.

Although complete restoration will not be fully realized until Jesus returns to establish a new heaven and a new earth (Rev. 21), there are moments of harmony between God, mankind, and creation. One glimpse of that peace this side of eternity is when Jesus walks out of the desert and begins His earthly ministry. Whereas Adam and Eve said yes to Satan's offer and surrendered the garden to decay, Jesus says no to Satan's every temptation. This decisive victory ushers in a season of hope and healing. Jesus calms storms, rebukes demons, and introduces peace everywhere He goes.

When Jesus invites the disciples to follow Him, He invites them into this same mission. In this letter to the Ephesians, the apostle Paul writes of the purpose of Christ's mission:

> For he himself is our peace, who has made the two groups one and has destroyed the barrier, the dividing wall of hostility, by setting aside in his flesh the law with its commands and regulations. His purpose was to create in himself one new humanity out of the two,

thus making peace, and in one body to reconcile both of them to God through the cross, by which he put to death their hostility. He came and preached peace to you who were far away and peace to those who were near. For through him we both have access to the Father by one Spirit. (Eph. 2:14–18)

Jesus invites all of us to join Him. When you surrender your life to the Prince of Peace, not only do you experience "peace . . . which surpasses all understanding" (Phil. 4:7 ESV), you also introduce His peace to a world that desperately needs it.

We don't have to look far to find tension in the world. Sometimes that world revolves around our own dinner table. Even among the fictional superhero teams, the Avengers and Justice League, we often see infighting as much as we see them fighting together for others. One of the heroes typically has to step up and remind his friends what's at stake if they don't learn to get along. But once they resolve their differences and focus on the mission, they are able to save the city, world, or universe (the stakes keep going up with each movie!).

I remember when the Chicago Bulls won their third consecutive championship. It was 1993, and I was sixteen years old. Driving home from work in a suburb of Chicago, I heard the announcer scream that John Paxson had just clinched the game with a three-point shot. The moment felt miraculous. The streets became a spontaneous block party. Rival gangs were hugging. Cats and dogs were getting married. Stingy uncles were picking up the tab. Fireworks were going up in the air rather than gunshots. Queen's song "We Are the Champions" was playing on the radio, on repeat.

For a few moments, everything seemed right with the world. It was one of those moments when you wanted to press pause. Tragically, peace never lasts on this side of eternity. Promises are broken. Treaties are violated. In fact, the celebration was overshadowed by conflict. Two people were tragically killed as parties turned into riots. Vehicles were set on fire. What should have been a time of great joy turned into a time of mourning as the city divided itself. Once again, Chicago needed people to come to its rescue.

I've been thinking about something the apostle Paul says to a young leader named Timothy: "Guard what has been entrusted to your care" (1 Tim. 6:20). How am I doing at protecting what God has placed under my care? How am I protecting my family, my friends, my church, my community, my gifts, my goals, my money, and my moments? When Paul says that we are to guard what has been entrusted to us, the word *entrusted* implies that what I have is truly *His*. God has graced me with all that I have and it requires guarding. How are you doing at protecting what God has placed under your care? Are you protecting your city?

I was told when I became a pastor that you don't just shepherd a church, you shepherd a city. I assumed that was an exaggeration until I found myself spiritually caring for people at the gym, coffeehouse, grocery store, and even the men's locker room. "Pastor Dan, will you pray for me? Give me advice? What do you think about this mole?" I've heard and seen things that should only be shared with doctors and those with a strong stomach and no gag reflex.

I was once called to visit an elderly woman in the hospital. She was in her eighties and heard about me through a relative. She had no home church, no community to support her in a time of need. I knew that she would most likely never come visit my congregation or listen to me preach. I still felt responsible to take the church to her.

When I walked into the room, I sat in the chair at the foot of her hospital bed and asked if there was anything I could pray for. She motioned toward the sheet over her legs and said, "You could pray for them to remove this catheter." They don't prepare you for those awkward moments in seminary. While that experience haunts me, and I no longer sit at the foot of the bed when I visit people in the hospital, I did pray for her and walked away knowing that I was probably the only expression of Jesus that came to visit her that day or any other day. She had been abandoned by family and friends.

While there are no comic book superheroes who protect Milwaukee or Chicago, I know that God has asked me and others to take on that role. We are to protect the poor, the elderly, the spiritually hungry, the addicted, the dying, the confused, the lost, and the little old ladies who confuse pastors for doctors. Ministry is messy.

You have a corner of the world that desperately needs your prayers, influence, time, love, and resources. How have you been doing at guarding what God has put into your hands? In the popular TV series *Green Arrow*, the title character is famous for telling people that they "have failed their city." I don't want to hear God say those words to me.

Nehemiah is famous for protecting and restoring the city of Jerusalem. He is one of my favorite leaders and has an entire book of the Bible named after him. The first seven chapters of his story are about building a wall. He takes the words "guard what has been placed under your care" very seriously.

Nehemiah traveled 1,500 miles to help protect the city of Jerusalem.[2] It's 1,200 miles from where I live in Wisconsin to Disney World. While I love the Magic Kingdom, I can't imagine traveling there on foot to help with a construction project. Especially if I'm anywhere nearby when people are singing "It's a Small World After All" or "Let It Go."

Even more impressive to me about Nehemiah's travels is that he was the cupbearer for the king. He was like chief chef at the White House. He was in a position of prestige and trust. He lived in the most powerful country in the world. The city where he dwelled was secure; there were no holes in their wall. It would have been easy for him to say that Jerusalem was not his problem. It's one thing to get concerned about a hole in your own wall but something entirely different to get concerned about the hole in other people's walls.

Sometimes you protect the city you're born in. At other times, you protect the city you're called to. Bruce Wayne is born within the city limits of Gotham. Clark Kent moved to Metropolis as an adult. God may use you where you are or He may call you to a city halfway around the world.

Nehemiah was like a second Joshua, because he was sent

to help take back what rightfully belonged to God's people. The book of Nehemiah can be divided into two sections, with the first six chapters focusing on rebuilding the wall and chapters 7 through 13 on rebuilding the people.[3] The idea of reading about Nehemiah rebuilding a wall may sound terribly boring. We don't normally get excited about people building walls. I like the Great Wall of China, but I wouldn't want to watch a whole movie about its construction. But when you realize the value of the wall around Jerusalem and the miraculous way in which God restored the wall that had been destroyed by Israel's enemies, and that it was finished in a record-breaking fifty-two days, reading about this construction project becomes inspiring.

In the ancient world, the wall was a nation or city's best defense. Without a protective wall, one didn't need to be a super villain to destroy a city. Any ambitious thief could put together a raiding party, grab some crude weapons, and rob the city. Building the wall was the first step toward protecting the city of Jerusalem. Its fence was its defense. The original wall was a few miles long. It had sat in ruin for over a hundred years, broken pieces piled at the bottom of a steep embankment. Jerusalem was surrounded by foreigners who did not want the wall rebuilt. Most of the people who would rebuild the wall were not construction workers, and they had no cranes to lift these chunks of wall, which were several hundred pounds. The situation seemed impossible.

When Nehemiah stood among a group of refugees and said that they were going to rebuild the wall around Jerusalem, I'm sure many of them laughed. We want to protect the city, but we often don't feel qualified. There is a phrase in Nehemiah chapter 3 that appears twenty times. The three words "next to him" are the secret to the wall getting built in a record fifty-two days. Chapter 3 is simply a list of all the people who helped rebuild the wall. It is like reading the credits after a movie (and not a Marvel movie where you get a cool bonus scene).

What is interesting about the people shoulder to shoulder is that most of them are not construction workers. Among the workers were priests, perfume makers, and a politician with his daughters. Any of them could have easily said that they didn't have the spiritual gift of building walls. They are not the top 2 percent of society; they are the 98 percent who are willing to place what is in their hands into God's hands. They are ordinary people accomplishing something extraordinary because they see the city as vulnerable and they are willing to do what they can to make a difference. Are you willing to do whatever it takes to make a difference?

It is our responsibility to work alongside God and to protect the corner He has put under our care. To be the salt of the earth and a light in the world. To pray for our neighbors. To live, love, and share the gospel. The story of Nehemiah drives this point home. There is a time for making things personal: "Fight for your families" (Neh. 4:14). Or in the words of Jesus, "whatever you did for one of the least of these . . . you did for me" (Matt. 25:40). Remember what's at stake if you don't fight. Nehemiah knows that it's harder to risk your life for nameless neighbors than it is for sons and daughters. He must make things personal.

> *I'm convinced that the greatest weapon the devil created was the recliner.*

What if people who need our help aren't part of our "family"? It's hard to fight for the "others." It's hard to love labels. When you see people as categories, like Muslim, Mormon, Democrat, Republican, LGBTQ, it's easier to turn a blind eye to their suffering. But when you see everyone as created in God's image, then we are more likely to have the conviction to leave our comfort zone and engage. I know I would take a bullet for my wife and three kids, but I would like to think I would take a bullet for a complete stranger too.

I find Edmund Burke's words challenging: "The only thing necessary for the triumph of evil is for good men to do nothing." I'm convinced that the greatest weapon the devil created was the recliner. Many a potential hero was disarmed by the promise of a Lay-Z-Boy. Comfort often trumps conviction. What will it take to get you off your chair?

A few years ago, I heard about a man whose wife left him for another man just before Christmas. They had young kids, and he was unemployed. I received an unexpected Christmas bonus, and my first thought was to use part of it to help them. I called my wife, and we agreed on an amount. We felt like a couple of Christmas elves shopping for those kids. When we gave them their gifts, you would have thought the family had won the Publishers Clearing House sweepstakes.

The next day, my wife was at work when she got a surprise bonus for the exact amount that we had just used to go shopping for that family. You can't outgive God. The city is full of people who need you to be their answer to prayer.

Historically, Spider-Man has been the most popular of the comic book heroes. He is called the *Amazing* Spider-Man for a reason. If I were going to be a superhero, it would probably be Spider-Man. We are both skinny and sarcastic, and we both look good in Spandex. Well, at least two out of those three is true.

When Peter Parker is bitten by a radioactive spider, he is given super strength, spider senses, and the ability to climb walls and swing between buildings. In spite of this newfound power, Peter Parker had no desire to be a hero. He initially used his gift to make money as a pro wrestler. When a thief runs past him, he has a chance to step up, save the day, and capture the bad guy. But he lets him go, figuring it isn't his problem. Later, Peter's Uncle Ben is gunned down by that same thief. If Spider-Man had intervened, he could have prevented his uncle's death. It's in that moment that his uncle utters the most famous comic book words, "With great power comes great responsibility."[4] This memorable statement echoes Jesus' words, "To whom much was given, of him much will be required" (Luke 12:48 ESV).

Peter must decide what he is going to do with the gifts he has been given. Is he going to use them for profit or to protect the city? We also must determine what we are going to do with the one and only life we have been given.

When one of my sons was little he asked me why God

didn't make people with superpowers. With my dad wisdom, I said God has given us the superpower of imagination. With our imagination, we can create airplanes so we can fly like Superman, submarines so we can go underwater like Aquaman, or race cars so we can travel fast like the Flash. He thought about that for a moment and said, "I think I'd rather have one of the other superpowers."

With our imagination, we can put a dent in world hunger, cure life-threatening illnesses, tear down prejudices, fix the economy, and hand our kids an even better future than we inherited. This is implied by the first commandment God ever gave. Shortly after God creates Adam and Eve, He tells them to "subdue [the earth]" (Gen. 1:28). That phrase means to "bring under control." Think about a teenager's bedroom. What happens if you don't give the frequent reminder to clean up their room? Things tend to drift toward chaos. One of our roles is to protect the world from getting out of control. This is what Jesus was getting at when He said that we "are the salt of the earth" (Matt. 5:13). Salt in the first century was used to keep food from spoiling. We are to help prevent moral decay. We are to fight for peace.

Protecting the city starts with protecting your character. God told Abraham that if He could find ten righteous people in Sodom, He would not destroy it. The city had become so corrupt that morality was a minority. God could not find even ten model citizens, so He was forced to level the city. What if God is looking at your community right now and saying, "If I can just find a handful of people totally committed to Me, we could turn this place around."

Do not underestimate your role. You may be one of the only people preventing your city from crumbling into chaos. D. L. Moody is credited with saying, "The world has yet to see what God can do with a man fully consecrated to him. By God's help, I aim to be that man." My prayer is that a generation of people would echo those words and rise up to protect the city.

Chapter 8

THE ORIGINAL DYNAMIC DUO

I magine on one side of the room is a whiteboard with a light bulb drawn on it. The picture represents an idea, a dream, a potential. On the other side of the room is an actual light bulb screwed into a lamp. In between the dream and reality is a gap. The way a dream goes from an idea to a reality is with the hands of volunteers. Men and women who are willing to step up and courageously say I'll use my time, talent, and treasure to have an impact on the lives of others. Thomas Edison said, "Genius is one percent inspiration, ninety-nine percent perspiration."[1] It was not just Edison's effort that made the light bulb a reality, it was the sweat of his very talented team.

It doesn't matter how soul-stirring, off-the-charts important that 1 percent of inspiration is if people don't work to make it become a reality. Martin Luther King Jr.'s dream of racial reconciliation, a day when people would be judged based on character rather than color, a day when America would be led by a black president, could never have been ignited without thousands of volunteers. Granted, we still have a long way to go. The Emancipation Proclamation changed laws but not hearts. But it will be ordinary brave men and women who will carry the dream forward. John F. Kennedy's dream to put a man on the moon never would have happened without engineers, scientists, and brave individuals willing to strap themselves into a rocket, hurtle through space, and achieve "one small step for man, one giant leap for mankind."

God's dream to impact the world with forgiveness, freedom, love, and healing could never be realized without the coming of Christ, His ministry and sacrifice, and the millions of volunteers who are willing to share in His mission and message. Right now, there are over 560 million Protestant Christians around the world.[2] They exist because of dedicated praying elders, mentoring youth workers, welcoming greeters, engaging teachers, and passionate worship leaders. The church has created hospitals, orphanages, art, architecture, and literature. It has fought against disease, poverty, human trafficking, and racism. All this has been made possible not just by the paid professionals but by the volunteers who were willing to put on their work gloves and lock arms with God.

If you are reading this book, you probably have access to clean water. Maybe you prefer it in the form of an energy drink, coffee, or a pumpkin spice latte, but you have the option to stay hydrated. In most developed parts of the world, it's easy to take water for granted. We can afford bottled water, hot showers, and summertime water balloon fights. According to the Water Project, in developing countries 80 percent of the illnesses are related to poor water conditions. One in five deaths of children under age five is caused by a water-related disease.[3]

Jesus states that if you serve and provide a cup of water in His name, you do it for Him (see Matt. 10:42). There are millions of people around the world who need that cup of water. This is not limited to cups of cold water but can include any act of service done in Christ's name.

There's a twenty-year-old in my church who helped make sure a village in Africa had access to water. The Gates Foundation will never approach him to join their list of billionaire donors. Most days he's not even a hundredaire much less a billionaire. While he doesn't have a big checkbook, he has a huge heart for charity. Our church was raising money to dig a well in Africa, and we were short one thousand dollars. This young man used his tax refund to fill in the gap. There are people on the other side of the planet that he will never meet this side of eternity who are staying hydrated and healthy because of his sacrificial gift.

There have been a lot of great dynamic duos: Batman and Robin; Captain America and Bucky; The Flash and Kid Flash; Green Arrow and Speedy; Thor and his hammer (who needs a partner when you have Mjolnir?).

*The greatest
dynamic duo
of all is
God and us,
Christ and
the church.*

The greatest dynamic duo of all is God and us, Christ and the church. God does not expect us to change the world alone. He wants us to piggyback on what He is already doing. Jesus is not retired; His ascension was not an escape plan. He's not sitting around eating angel food cake and listening to harp music. Jesus is at work, and not just on Easter and Christmas but right now.

The title for the New Testament book "Acts of the Apostles" was created by historians. A better title though would be "Acts of Jesus through the Apostles." I make this claim because of what Luke, the author of Acts, says: "In my former book, Theophilus, I wrote about all that Jesus began to do and to teach" (Acts 1:1). In Luke's mind, Jesus didn't stop teaching and doing just because He ascended to heaven. In fact, Jesus' activity grew exponentially because of His new address.

Jesus puts it this way, "Very truly I tell you, whoever believes in me will do the works I have been doing, and they will do even greater things than these, because I am going to the Father" (John 14:12). Notice the word *greater*. Jesus is arguably the most influential person in human history. While we still struggle to predict the weather, He could stop a storm with a simple command. While we still haven't found a cure for the common cold, He healed diseases

The Original Dynamic Duo

as devastating as leprosy with a touch. How could a person possibly surpass His greatness? I don't think this means we will all walk on water and empty funeral homes. When Jesus walked this earth, He was limited in how many people He could touch, talk to, and heal. He never traveled more than two hundred miles from home and He carried out His ministry within the same number of hours in a day we have.

When He ascended into heaven, He unleashed the Holy Spirit. Through the power of the Holy Spirit, we can become His hands and feet. His greatness grew exponentially. As His body, we ensure that Jesus' impact has gone from the villages of Israel to the entire planet as people follow His lead. In the words often accredited to Teresa of Ávila[4]:

> Christ has no body but yours,
> No hands, no feet on earth but yours,
> Yours are the eyes with which he looks
> Compassion on this world,
> Yours are the feet with which he walks to do good,
> Yours are the hands, with which he blesses all the world.

We can see God's desire for partnership all the way back in the first book of the Bible: "Now no shrub had yet appeared on the earth and no plant had yet sprung up, for the LORD God had not sent rain on the earth and there was no one to work the ground" (Gen. 2:5). Notice that fruitfulness is dependent on God sending rain and volunteers working the ground. This theme will continue throughout Scripture. In fact, Paul says that as the church, we are "co-workers" with God (1 Cor.

3:9). We don't just work for God; we work *with* God.

God isn't just a compassionate CEO that we report to. When I worked at the cleaning service, the boss had his office on the second floor, back corner. I worked *for* him; I never worked *with* him. He never grabbed a plunger and helped me unclog a toilet. He never grabbed the Windex and helped me clean the windows. He never grabbed a trash can and helped collect garbage.

God, on the other hand, wants to work with us. You see, God is already at work in the world, at work in your world, and He can't wait for you to join Him. Listen to the conversation between God and the prophet Isaiah: "Then I heard the voice of the Lord saying, 'Whom shall I send? And who will go for us?' And I said, 'Here am I. Send me!'" (Isa. 6:8). What if those five words were on the lips and hearts of all who call themselves Christ followers? What if, "Here am I. Send me," was our superhero catchphrase? There are a lot of famous superhero catchphrases:

> Up, up and away!
> My Spidey senses are tingling.
> Hulk smash!
> Flame on!
> Shazam!

One of the most powerful phrases Jesus spoke was, "Thy will be done" (Matt. 6:10 KJV). Those four words changed not only history but eternity. Jesus was hours away from rescuing billions of lives from death and the devil. He knew that to offer life He must experience death. While firefighters snatch people from burning buildings while trying to not get burned, and the Coast Guard rescues people from the water while trying not to drown, Jesus knew the only way to rescue lives from the consequences of sin was through the cross. There could be no forgiveness or freedom without a sacrifice.

We know that Jesus, being both God and man, saw the cross long before the garden. He told His closest friends, "We are going up to Jerusalem, and the Son of Man will be delivered over to the chief priests and the teachers of the law. They will condemn him to death and will hand him over to the Gentiles to be mocked and flogged and crucified" (Matt. 20:18–19). There's a rare courage to see how you are going to die and intentionally march toward it—to choose sacrifice over self-preservation, to trade all the things you could have done with your life to rescue people who will never be able to fully thank you. What worship could match His worthiness? I think about the young soldiers getting off the boats on the beaches of Normandy or the firefighters running into the Twin Towers on 9/11. Jesus walked toward Jerusalem when most people would have run toward the other side of the planet.

Jesus watched as the sun set and knew that His life was fading as well. He was on His knees in the garden of Gethsemane mustering the courage to face the cross. Strategically, He had had one last meal with His friends. Perhaps He was holding their faces in His mind, knowing that they would never enjoy a meal in eternity together without this sacrificial step. In desperation, He prayed, "Father, if you are willing, take this cup from me" (Luke 22:42). There is tension between Jesus' divinity and His humanity. His divinity knows that the only way to save mankind is to face the cross. His humanity desperately wishes there was another way, a plan B. Imagine the pressure of knowing all of creation is lost without this final heroic act. There is no sidekick to take His place. The first words God ever spoke were "let there be light." Once again, darkness has descended. This time, to bring light it will not be through His words but His wounds. When the sun rose Easter morning, an even brighter light was unleashed as Jesus rose from the dead. That light shines through thousands of years and billions of places around the globe as each of us reflect His life and character.

We all experience a microcosm of these moments when our dream for our life doesn't align with our destiny, our wants don't align with God's will. In those moments, we have to decide whose will we are going to live for. Living a "Thy will be done" kind of life is not always easy. As a dad, my kids are my sanctuary. When life feels out of control, they are my equilibrium. I don't understand what a friend of mine calls the "Houdini dad." They bring a child into the world and then disappear halfway through "the show." Yet one in three kids in the United States grows up without a dad at home.[5]

I heard the story of a man whose wife cheated on him, became pregnant, and then let him believe he was the father. Eventually, he learned the truth. On reality TV, when the envelope is pulled out, and the talk show host says "you are not the father," some of the dads react angrily. Instead, this man chose that moment to continue raising the child as his own. In spite of the reminder of betrayal, he chose to pray, "Thy will be done" and take God's path of forgiveness. To me, that's heroic.

Before Jesus could utter the words "it is finished," He had to pray "Thy will be done." The only way Jesus can authentically pray these words in death is that He lived them in life. They guided Him when He chose to shrink down to the size of an embryo and entrust His life to a teenage girl. They guided Him when He grew up in obscurity and poverty, although as King of the universe, He deserves palaces and servants. They guided Him when He left family and home to live wherever someone was kind enough to let Him stay. They guided Him when He marched into the desert to go toe-to-toe with evil incarnate. They guided Him when He risked becoming a social pariah by eating with the outcasts. They guided Him when He went against the grain and chose mercy over following pharisaic rules. They guided Him when He skipped a meal, sacrificed sleep, and gave up personal space to heal one more person. They guided Him once more as He chose the cross and saving souls rather than pursuing self-preservation. Jesus' entire life was defined by those four words, "Thy will be done."

If we want to have the greatest possible impact on this world, we must live those words as well. The first time I breathed those words was in a trailer in the middle of the Wisconsin woods. I was eighteen years old, and I was tired of living as a moral maverick. I had lived a "my will be done" kind of life, and it had left me empty. That night with tears streaming down my face I prayed, "God, You can take my life. I'm Yours." I had no idea what that prayer would mean for my future.

I have had the privilege of helping people experience God's grace and forgiveness for the first time. Every time I baptize someone I think back to my "Thy will be done" prayer. Every time I help restore a marriage or help a person find freedom from addiction, I think of that "Thy will be done" prayer. Every time I offer a meal to a homeless person or visit someone in jail, I think of that "Thy will be done" prayer. Every time someone talks about how their perspective on life and God has shifted because of the words I've shared, I think back to that "Thy will be done" prayer. Who is waiting for you to start praying "Thy will be done"?

> *Heroes pray and practice a "Thy will be done" kind of life.*

C. S. Lewis once said, "There are only two kinds of people in the end: those who say to God, 'Thy will be done,' and those to whom God says, in the end, '*Thy* will be done.'"[6] Heroes pray and practice a "Thy will be done" kind of life.

Are you ready to join Jesus in His adventure to save souls? Are you ready to join the greatest dynamic duo ever?

Chapter 9

JUSTICE COMES DOWN TO *JUST US*

We live in a world where heroes can become villains and villains can become heroes.

No one's character is immutable or unchanging. A badge doesn't always mean "good guy." Being a priest or pastor doesn't guarantee godliness. Dog tags don't guarantee patriotism. On the flip side, failure doesn't have to be final. Prisoners can be released and become model citizens. Addicts can recover and become great parents. Prostitutes can escape exploitation and lead the abused toward healing. I once saw a tattoo that sums this up well: "All saints have a past. All sinners have a future."

Before I got my master's degree, I was a high school

dropout. Before I became a pastor, I was a drug dealer. Before I ran with God, I ran from Him. I've experienced mercy and metamorphosis firsthand. I used to sell dope and now I serve hope.

Although I grew up in church, the ways of the church did not grow within me. I was content to praise on Sunday and party on Friday. It didn't take long until the Friday night parties infested the rest of the week. Soon I was skipping class and work to chase another high. My descent started with recreational drugs and spiraled into harder drugs. At one point, I sold drugs out of my parents' house a block away from the police station. It was only by God's grace and my family's prayers that I escaped without jail time or permanent brain damage.

One of the things that attracts me to superhero stories is that most of the characters go through a profound change. When Bruce Banner is exposed to gamma radiation, he morphs from a 128-pound scientist to a 1,400-pound mean, green fighting machine as the Hulk. Talk about a growth spurt. When Peter Parker is bitten by a radioactive spider, he goes from an awkward teenager with pimples and a squeaky voice to a superhero with the ability to crawl across walls and swing through Manhattan on his spider webs.

More intriguing than the enhanced powers is the enhanced perspective. These larger-than-life characters experience dramatic shifts from selfishness to servanthood.

When I embraced Christ's leadership and love, it changed the polarity of my life. My true north flipped from "What can I get from this relationship?" to "What can I give?" As an addict, I had no problem stealing from "friends" and endangering my family by inviting shady people into our home. I wasn't concerned about the ulcers I was giving my mom. I didn't lose sleep over the headache I gave my boss when I wouldn't show up to work. I didn't think twice about the bad example I was setting for my younger sister. I was narcissistic and self-absorbed—a villain.

In a popular anti-drug commercial at the time, a person held up a pristine, white egg as a voiceover explained that "this is your brain." The egg was then cracked open and dropped into a hot pan as the voice continued, "This is your brain on drugs." I would often roll my eyes at that commercial, hungrier for omelets than sobriety. But in retrospect I can say that when you're on drugs, it's not just the brain that gets scrambled, it's the priorities and relationships.

Jesus changed all that. When I said yes to Jesus' salvation, I also said yes to His servant's heart. The first thing I wanted to do was help teenagers avoid the same mistakes I had made. I was no longer intoxicated by the pursuit of happiness; instead, I was in love with the pursuit of helpfulness (which ironically made me happy). I would lay my head on my pillow at night and dream about ways I could better serve others. The seismic shift in my priorities was nothing less than miraculous.

Experiencing this shift is one reason the hero's journey resonates with me. The hero's identity crisis becomes an identity chrysalis. He or she emerges with purpose, vision, and courage. These heroes realize that sometimes justice comes down to *just us*. We can't wait for someone else to act first. You

> *Heroes realize that sometimes justice comes down to just us.*

can't delegate to others what God has delegated to you. There comes a moment when you must get off your knees in prayer and take a stand.

Jesus challenged His disciples to do just that. In the book of Matthew, we read of one such occasion when He had compassion on the crowds of people who were "harassed and helpless, like sheep without a shepherd" (Matt. 9:36). Listen to Jesus' words to His disciples: "The harvest is plentiful but the workers are few. Ask the Lord of the harvest, therefore, to send out workers into his harvest field" (Matt. 9:37–38). I can just picture the disciples enthusiastically agreeing with Jesus: "Yep, things are pretty messed up. Someone should do something about that. We will make this a top shelf prayer request. We won't get off our knees until God convinces someone to get out there."

But then in the very next verse Jesus essentially says *that it's easy to pray and pray, but are you willing to pave the way?* He charged them to take action themselves: "Jesus called his twelve disciples to him and gave them authority to drive out impure spirits and to heal every disease and sickness" (Matt. 10:1). In other words, don't pray for God to intervene unless you're willing to be a part of the solution. Again, justice sometimes comes down to just us.

While I was working on this section, a young lady called me asking for prayer. She had been abused by a teacher when she was a young girl. She had never come forward because of her embarrassment and hurt, but she found out that this guy was teaching young kids again, even though he had been previously accused of sexual misconduct with another minor. She knew that she needed to be a voice for the voiceless. As a new mother she looked down at her son and knew that she had to do what she could to make the world a safer place. Willing to face fear, shame, guilt, and a past she would rather bury, she stepped up and spoke out. Sometimes justice comes down to just us.

No one else is going to stand up or speak up. You can cower among the crowd or raise your voice.

David had to stand up to the giant.
Esther had to stand up to the king.
Paul had to stand up to the religious leaders.
What are you willing to stand up for?

Richard Stearns, the current CEO for World Vision, was willing to stand up. He was the CEO of Lenox when he received the invitation to do something about global poverty and injustice. He lived in a ten-bedroom house on five acres of land, drove a Jaguar, and took first-class trips to Paris, Tokyo, and London. He was living the American dream when God invited him to the kingdom dream. He walked away from a twenty-three-year career and took a 75 percent cut in pay. On the day he was supposed to make his decision, he was offered a CEO position at another company where he was guaranteed to make 25 to 50 million dollars, but he chose World Vision instead.[1] Now 4.1 million children benefit from his choice to stand up.[2]

One of the inspiring things about the X-Men series is how Charles Xavier starts a school for mutants. In a world where these kids with powers are looked at as freaks, he sees their potential. He teaches them a lesson far more valuable than social studies and science; he teaches them that different doesn't have to mean defective. They are all beautiful no matter their fur, claws, speed, or skill. It would have been enough for him to use his telepathic powers to help others, but he goes far beyond that by opening his home to those who were often abandoned by friends and family.

So many children worldwide grow up with abusive or absent parents. There are close to 140 million children worldwide who are orphans.[3] A woman in my church took in three of her grandkids when their mom and dad were not reliable; mom was in jail and dad was on drugs. While many grandparents have joked that the best part of having grandkids is the ability to send them home after spoiling them and pumping them full of sugar, this grandma took on the full-time job of being a mom for the second time. She has been the safety net for those children. Tragically, their mom was killed in a car accident two weeks after getting out of jail and their dad was killed in a hit and run the same week. Grandma has been the bulletproof vest taking the brunt of the shots aimed in their direction. They have still experienced the blows of heartache but not as forcefully as they would have if their committed grandmother had not been there.

My oldest son recently appeared in a production of the musical *Annie*, which is the story of an orphan girl who gets adopted by a self-made billionaire. Before the school production began, a gentleman got up and talked about foster care. He said that there are twice as many kids in our city who need foster care as there are homes available. He read the verse in James where it says that the kind of religion that God gets fired up about is taking care of orphans and widows (see James 1:27). So, he and his wife stepped up and adopted one of those kids.

It made me think about a family in my church that has adopted nine kids after raising three children of their own. That's more than the old woman who lived in a shoe. I'm sure you're familiar with that nursery rhyme. The Christian version of that poem goes like this:

> There was an old woman
> Who lived in a shoe,
> She had so many children,
> And loved them all, too.
> She said, "Thank you, Lord Jesus,
> For sending them bread,"
> Then kissed them all gladly
> And sent them to bed.[4]

But the original story had a little different take on a house full of screaming kids:

There was an old woman who lived in a shoe,
She had so many children she didn't know what to do;
She gave them some broth without any bread;
She whipped them all soundly and put them to bed.[5]

In a world where many kids face the second version of that story, this family fought to be the first—to be a sanctuary for children and to create a space where they feel secure and significant. Sometimes being a hero means opening your heart and home. We are surrounded by examples of heroic acts, actions that might not be seen by social media but are seen by the Savior. Jesus once said, "If anyone gives even a cup of cold water to one of these little ones who is my disciple . . . that person will certainly not lose their reward" (Matt. 10:42).

God sees.
God knows.
God rewards.

While it is tempting to complain that we have nothing to offer, if the world was boiled down to a hundred people:

50 of them would live on less than two dollars a day.
Only 7 of them would have a college degree.
Only 22 would own or share a computer.[6]

According to these standards, most of us have margin in our lives to help others. God has not blessed you financially so you can fulfill your own wishes. God told Abraham, "I will bless you and make your name great, *so that* you will be a blessing" (Gen. 12:2 ESV). In the same way, your gifts, intelligence, experiences, and financial resources are not just for you but also for the people God wants to bless through you.

What if being a hero is not about the grand gesture but rather it's a lifetime of looking out for others? What if being a hero is as simple as holding a door open for an elderly person, attending your child's musical, or giving the cashier a heads-up that they accidentally handed you too much change? What if being a hero means letting a car merge into your lane, paying for the coffee of the person next in line, or simply changing the toilet paper (the right way, of course)? Kindness, integrity, and love are contagious. After God asks Cain where his missing brother Abel is, Cain poses a very telling question, "Am I my brother's keeper?" (Gen. 4:9). The answer is an emphatic "Yes!" Being a hero has less to do with superpowers and more to do with having a servant's heart. In the comics, super villains have all the same powers as the good guys; the difference is their lack of concern for humanity. They use what they must to enrich themselves at the expense of others. Powers don't make a hero, character does. A lifetime of seemingly small and insignificant acts is what will make this world a better place, not just the stories that grab national attention.

Batman said to Commissioner Gordon, "A hero can be anyone. Even a man doing something as simple and reassuring as putting a coat around a young boy's shoulders to let him know that the world hadn't ended."[7] Sometimes it's just the smallest act of kindness that makes all the difference in the world. In the words of D. L. Moody, "I am only one, but I am one. I cannot do everything, but I can do something. And that which I can do, by the grace of God, I will do."

Sometimes justice comes down to: Just us.

Chapter 10

A TRAGIC BEGINNING

While Heath Ledger's Joker is famous for the line, "Why so serious?" I never took Batman very seriously as a kid. My uncle used to sing, "Jingle bells, Batman smells, Robin laid an egg, the Batmobile lost its wheel, and the Joker got away." He was a real classy kind of guy.

The only Batman I knew was played by Adam West. He looked more like the entertainment for a kid's birthday party than someone villains would fear. His sidekick, Robin, would deliver cheesy lines like, "Holy strawberries, Batman! We're in a jam." With writing like that I'm not sure why the show never won an Emmy. When Batman or Robin threw a punch, a bubble would appear on the screen with words like "Sock!" or "Pow!" And if it was really hard it was, "Kapow!"

It wasn't until I saw writer-director Christopher Nolan's film trilogy that I began to take Batman seriously. What intrigued me most was Batman's tragic backstory. We've all heard about how young Bruce Wayne witnessed his parents' murder; it's one of comic books' most famous deaths. A few days later, young Bruce makes this vow: "By the spirit of my parents I swear to avenge their deaths, by spending the rest of my life warring on all criminals."[1] Tragedy transformed a boy into Batman.

Pastor and author Charles Swindoll once said, "I am convinced that life is 10 percent what happens to me and 90 percent how I react to it."[2] Two people can go through the same tragic events and have very different responses. Not everyone is going to put on tights and a mask and fight against criminals like young Bruce did. We all go through tragedy, but not all of us *grow* through tragedy.

When I think about Batman's tragic beginnings, I can't help but think about a non-comic superhero—a young man in the Old Testament named Joseph. He received impressive visions about his future and believed God would carry them out. But Joseph was betrayed by his brothers, the people he should have been able to trust most. They sold him into slavery for twenty pieces of silver, which was about two years' wages for a common shepherd[3] (see Gen 37:28). From there, Joseph's life seemed to spiral out of control. He went from slavery to jail. It seemed like his life was drifting further and further away from all that God promised him. But through a series of events, Joseph found himself elevated to one of the most powerful positions in Egypt. Years later, because of famine in Canaan, his brothers traveled to Egypt to buy food. There they encountered Joseph, who graciously said, "Do not be distressed and do not be angry with yourselves for selling me here, because it was to save lives that God sent me ahead of you" (Gen. 45:5). As Joseph discovered, God can take some of the most horrendous things this world can throw at us and bring good out of them. God knows how to transform tragedy into triumph.

Most people have a scar or two. How many scars do you have?

If you went to the police to report a crime you witnessed, they would want you to describe what the criminal looked like. One of the things the detective might ask is if they have any visible tattoos, piercings, or scars, anything that would help identify the accused. Some people are known for their scars.

Many moms have scars from giving birth.
Soldiers have scars from going to war.
Kids have scars from falling from beds, bikes, and trees.

I have a scar on the corner of one eye from falling on the corner of a table as a child. I have a scar on the corner of the other eye from a TV that fell on me. Growing up, if I was going to hit something it was going to be my head. I'm surprised my face doesn't look like Sloth from *The Goonies*.

I was sitting next to my son the other day, and I was noticing all of his scars. He has a lot of scars for a teenager. Each of them represent pain, trauma, long nights, and the big bills that came along with that. Coincidentally, his scars appeared about the same time as my gray hairs. Each of them are reminders of a moment when he was wounded. He's no longer unblemished like he was as a newborn baby. He has been marked by his experiences in the world. Scars almost always bookmark a story.

Shortly after His death, Jesus reappeared to His followers. "A week later his disciples were in the house again, and Thomas was with them. Though the doors were locked, Jesus came and stood among them and said, 'Peace be with you!' Then he said to Thomas, 'Put your finger here; see my hands. Reach out your hand and put it into my side. Stop doubting and believe.' Thomas said to him, 'My Lord and my God!'" (John 20:26–28).

What's interesting to me is that although Jesus had a glorified body—He's been given some serious upgrades including the ability to walk through a wall and ascend into the air—He still has scars. In John's heavenly vision in the book of Revelation, he describes Jesus as "the Lamb who was slain" (Rev. 5:12; 13:8). I think Jesus' scars were visible because of what they would communicate to His disciples and to us. While every scar tells a story, His scars transform our story.

When kids dream of being a superhero, they envision flying, invincibility, and having the power to stop the enemy. The world's greatest hero rose into the air during the ascension, He was invincible until the cross, and He performed dozens of miracles. But none of these things were His greatest achievement. He rescued billions of lives through an act of unimaginable sacrifice. Five hundred years before Jesus' birth, Isaiah foreshadowed the kind of hero Jesus the Messiah would be: "Surely he took up our pain and bore our suffering, yet we considered him punished by God, stricken by him, and afflicted. But he was pierced for our transgressions, he was crushed for our iniquities; the punishment that brought us peace was on him, and by his wounds we are healed" (Isa. 53:4–5).

While Superman flies in with a cape, Jesus knelt with a servant's towel to wash the disciples' feet. While Thor uses a hammer to advance peace, Jesus bore the nails of the cross to secure our peace. While X-Men's founding member Jean Grey/Phoenix wields nearly unlimited power, Jesus set aside His omnipotent power to dwell among humans. While comic book heroes save the day, Jesus Christ died to save us forever. His death brought us life. His rejection guarantees our acceptance. His darkest hour ushered in our brightest day.

This doesn't mean that following Jesus makes us immune to the world's problems. This side of eternity, we won't empty every hospital, shut down the food pantries, cancel the psychology appointments, and transform funeral homes into theme parks. But at the cross, each swing of the hammer and crack of the whip sent an echo, reverberating throughout the ages, crescendoing in eternity. Perfection is coming.

We won't experience absolute healing until we take our last breath here and our first breath in heaven. But through Jesus' wounds, we have an eternal hope. As many theologians have pointed out, the kingdom of God is and is to come. In eternity there will be no more death, disease, disaster, or doubt. But while we wait for perfection, miracles spill over into the here and now. While only Jesus' wounds bring salvation, sometimes God uses our wounds—emotional scars, physical scars, even spiritual scars—to heal others.

Some wounds go deeper than others. I can't imagine anything more tragic than experiencing the death of a child—no one should outlive their kid. My friend Michele Batz suffered this tragedy. Her healthy, fun-loving son, Cory, started experiencing flu-like symptoms, but upon further testing, it was discovered he had cancer. Despite a valiant fight, optimism, and courage, Cory died while he was in high school. Many parents would have given up on life. Some of Cory's final words to his mom were that he knew where he was going when he died and that he didn't want his death to ruin her life. Michele and her husband have used this heart-wrenching experience as a catalyst to help other families who have gone through similar tragedies. Through their nonprofit, Cory's Project,[4] they share their story and raise funds for Children's Hospital in Milwaukee where their son was treated.

When I first met Michele, I didn't know her last name. The Sunday we were having her speak at church, the theme was about the comic book character Batman's tragic backstory and the life of the biblical hero Joseph. When I connected the dots, I said to her, "It's ironic that your name is Batz, and this week is about Batman." Michele said, "What a God wink. Cory was always known as Batz-man." Since the loss of Cory, God has used Michele's emotional scars to help thousands of people.

Sometimes God uses pain as a push to get us to bring

healing to a hurting world. There are times when what looks like "bad luck" can actually be an event God uses to change lives. Although Joseph was sold into slavery and sent to jail, God positioned him to save two nations, Egypt and Israel. God allowed persecution to break out against the first-century church, which catapulted them into the rest of the world: "On that day a great persecution broke out against the church at Jerusalem, and all except the apostles were scattered throughout Judea and Samaria" (Acts 8:1). Paul was shipwrecked and then bitten by a snake, which provided him with an opportunity to heal several people on an island called Malta.

For the first eight chapters of the book of Acts, the early church was centralized in Jerusalem. They were experiencing local miracles and explosive growth. People were excited about this new teaching. The meetings were energetic. Spiritually homeless people were running back to God. The generosity was contagious. Stomachs were being filled and bills were being paid. Jerusalem was at a fever pitch. But God's vision was bigger than one city or one people group. The gospel was intended to be contagious; it was meant to move beyond ground zero. John says it well: "For God so loved the *world*" (John 3:16). In order for the world to experience that love, the early converts needed a little nudge. Like a mother bird pushes her baby out of the nest, so God motivated His people to spread their wings.

God used pain to push. What is God trying to use to push you?

When we have endured pain, especially when it's not a

consequence of our sin, the temptation can be to grow bitter rather than grow better. How do we keep from growing bitter? Bitterness is like confetti: once it gets on you, it's hard to get off.

Let me share how my family battles bitterness. I turned forty last year, and for my birthday, my wife threw me a funeral. She called it a FUN-eral, but it was only fun for the people throwing it. It was a surprise party, complete with a large memorial picture of me at the front of the sanctuary, everyone dressed in black, and a very tall teenager from our church who dressed as the Grim Reaper. Each person took turns celebrating and roasting me. When my best friend got up, someone from the crowd yelled, "He loved you, man!" To which my friend responded, "I kind of liked him too. He was like my seventh or eighth closest friend." I know who is not invited to speak at my real funeral someday.

While we buried the first forty years of my life, little did I know that I was also burying the ability to eat whatever I want. That year I developed several allergies to food. I can no longer eat eggs, vanilla, brewer's yeast, chocolate, and several other things (if I listed them all, this would look like the ingredients on the side of an unhealthy cereal box). On most days, I feel like a diabetic living in a gingerbread house. I struggle with giving up some of my favorite foods. Why do my taste buds and digestive tract have to be at war with each other?

Because of these allergies, I have suffered severe problems with my stomach and have had to have my esophagus dilated because I was having trouble swallowing. Keep in mind my family already shoulders a lot medically, including my wife's degenerating eyesight and hearing. My oldest has had three procedures, and my youngest was in the ICU for the first five days of his life. So my struggles felt like too much. Why one more medical expense, one more headache?

It would be easy to complain about all the injustice and to let bitterness take over. But we choose to fight bitterness by fighting for joy. We hold tight to the gospel. Like a person who has fallen over the side of a cliff, we cling to the promise of Romans 8:28 as if it's the branch that's saving us from the unforgiving ground below: "And we know that in all things God works for the good of those who love him, who have been called according to his purpose."

As followers of Christ, this world is the only hell we will ever know.

We don't naively think any of these medical setbacks are good things, but we trust that God as the greatest recycler can repurpose our pain. As followers of Christ, this world is the only hell we will ever know. We look forward to a day when my wife can see clearly and I can eat a pound of chocolate chip cookies. While we don't always understand why, we know that when God makes all things new, everything will be clearer from an eternal perspective. In the words of John Milton, "The mind is its own place, and in itself can make a heaven of hell, a hell of heaven." We prayerfully ask God to transform our thoughts into His thoughts—to help us see even our pain through His eyes, to make a heaven out of hell. We don't always get this right. We have days filled with tears, doubt, and complaints. But in the days we get it right, joy wins and bitterness sits in the corner with a black eye.

A tragic beginning can lead to a triumphant ending. God often uses wounded healers. God wants to bring purpose out of your pain, triumph out of your tragedy.

Chapter 11

WHAT'S IN YOUR UTILITY BELT?

All superheroes have unique powers or tools that help them save the day.

Superman is faster than a speeding bullet.

The Martian Manhunter can read minds.

Wasp can fly, and she had mad leadership skills. (Not just anyone could lead the Avengers.)

And Batman can throw bat boomerangs. That only seems fair.

What is in your hands? I'm not referring to the latte or cellphone you may be holding. Rather, what gifts, talents, or skills has God invested in you that could be used to make a difference in the world? Maybe you feel as useless as a sidekick's sidekick . . . like you don't have anything of significance to offer.

Let me ask another question, which may seem unrelated. Have you ever worn a fanny pack? In the 1980s, men and women wore a mini purse on a belt around their waist. There's a picture of the famous wrestler, Dwayne "The Rock" Johnson, wearing one. It's one of the few times where he doesn't look very tough . . . not that I would say that to his face. Fanny packs were great for carrying your keys, sunglasses, lip balm, and wallet, especially on vacation or while enjoying Six Flags or a Disney resort.

1960s Batman essentially wore a fanny pack, but he called it a utility belt. It contained grapple guns, gas pellets, lock picks, and lozenges to help with his raspy voice. The Caped Crusader made sure that he always carried the tools with him that he would need for whatever mission he might stumble upon. I have often wished I had a utility belt full of strategic tools—a pacifier when someone is whining like a baby; an interpreter to help me understand what my wife is feeling; a stash of snacks for when I'm feeling "hangry." You know, just the essentials.

According to the apostle Paul, God has equipped all of us with a "utility belt" of sorts. Before our parents ever saw us on an ultrasound screen, God saw every challenge and opportunity that we would ever face. "We are God's handiwork, created in Christ Jesus to do good works, which God prepared in advance for us to do" (Eph. 2:10). You already have what you need. Where God guides, He provides. This is what God is hinting at when He asks Moses, "What is that in your hand?" (Ex. 4:2).

Israel had been in slavery for over four hundred years. God told Moses that He had heard the cries of His people. I picture Moses raising the roof at the thought of God flexing His muscles to rescue them. But his enthusiasm may have faded quickly when God followed up with "I am sending you" (Ex. 3:10). Poor Moses probably thought something along these lines: *What? You have had four hundred years to come up with a plan and Your brilliant idea is to send me? I'm an eighty-year-old shepherd, and You want me to go toe-to-toe with the most powerful nation in the world and convince them to let their free labor just walk away?*

God countered Moses's excuses with a fascinating question that is very tweet-worthy: "What is that in your hand?"

Moses simply answered, "A staff."

All Moses had to offer is a stick. In Moses's hand, the stick could lead sheep, fight small animals, or scratch his own back. While a stick in a kid's hands has all kinds of potential, it's not the weapon of choice to go free a bunch of slaves from the hands of the most powerful person on the planet. Fortunately for Moses and us, God has never been limited by our resources, but we limit ourselves by our responses. We must ask ourselves before we take an inventory of what's in our hands whether we are willing to place whatever it is into the hands of God.

"The LORD said, 'Throw it on the ground.' Moses threw it on the ground and it became a snake, and he ran from it"

> When we place what's in our hands into God's hands, the ordinary becomes extraordinary.

(Ex. 4:2–3). In God's hands, Moses would go on to use this stick to part the Red Sea, bring water out of a rock, and defeat the Amalekite army. When we place what's in our hands into God's hands, the ordinary becomes extraordinary.

When my oldest was eleven, he had surgery on his knee. He was supposed to stay off Franken-knee (the name we gave it because of the huge scar) for a few weeks. Halloween was only a couple of weeks after the surgery, so he was bummed to miss out on trick or treating. My father-in-law heard about the dilemma and converted a wheelchair into a tank. My son went from the potential of missing out to having the coolest costume on the streets that night. Police stopped us to take pictures, families gave him extra candy, and everyone assumed I made it, and I didn't correct them. (Just kidding, my father-in-law got the well-deserved credit.) All it took was a little creativity and some cardboard and Papa became a hero.

A friend of mine pastors a church in Wisconsin, and each spring they host A Night to Remember Prom for teens and young adults with special needs. They roll out a red carpet, set up "paparazzi" to take pictures, and treat their guests like celebrities. The volunteers do a great job of making those who feel invisible feel seen. Add some lights in an exciting venue with a DJ to play some music and a night is created that will be forever remembered by all who attend.

What experiences, education, gifts, or talents has God placed in your hands to help others? Maybe you feel like all you can offer the world is a stick.

But I'm always surprised at how many talented individuals feel insecure. Do you have a hidden talent? Some of the best singers will never make it from the shower to the stage. Is there a valuable experience in your past? People often waste life lessons because they are too embarrassed or ashamed to share. In recovery groups, it is often said, "hiding never leads to healing." That healing can refer to the one hiding or the people who could benefit from hearing their story.

Are we willing to offer what we have no matter how seemingly insignificant? We need to understand that no one is born without unique gifts. While we may not see the potential in the talents we possess, God sees miracles. Stop focusing on what you don't have, and start surrendering what you do have.

In 1 Kings 17, we read about a destitute woman who had to learn this lesson from the prophet Elijah. She was poor. She had only enough food for one last meal. In fact, she was ready to feed herself and her son and then planned to lie down and die. Following the Lord's instructions, Elijah simply asked her for some water and bread. The widow said, "I don't have any bread—only a handful of flour in a jar and a little olive oil in a jug" (1 Kings 17:12). You might expect Elijah to empathize and say, "The situation is even worse than I expected. What you have sounds more like a white elephant gift than the ingredients for a miracle." But instead Elijah encourages her to use what is in her hands:

> Elijah said to her, "Don't be afraid. Go home and do as you have said. But first make a small loaf of bread for me from what you have and bring it to me, and then make something for yourself and your son. For this is what the LORD, the God of Israel, says: 'The jar of flour will not be used up and the jug of oil will not run dry until the day the LORD sends rain on the land.'" She went away and did as Elijah had told her. So there was food every day for Elijah and for the woman and her family. For the jar of flour was not used up and the jug of oil did not run dry, in keeping with the word of the LORD spoken by Elijah. (1 Kings 17:13–16)

"Nothing at all" became more than enough.

The story about Elijah and the widow is a reminder that we often overlook the treasure in our own home. We are praying for God to send us a miracle, but He's waiting for us to offer up what we already have. Before we look out the window jealously believing that if we just had that one thing all of our problems would be solved, we should ask God to reveal to us what He has already placed within our own "house."

In 2013, while a man was demolishing some walls in his home during a renovation, he discovered old newspapers and an original Superman comic book that had been used for insulation. He knew if he sold the old comic that had been used to keep his house warm, he could afford a new house. The comic ended up being sold for $175,000.[1] This treasure was in his house, and he hadn't even realized it. I was so tempted to go home and punch a hole in my wall when I read that story. I'm confident all I would find is a bloody knuckle and disappointment.

What has God blessed you with that you are not recognizing or utilizing? When we take what's in our "house," and we use it to build God's house, something powerful happens.

What's in your hands? In the next few chapters we are going to talk about gifts we all have in our possession.

Chapter 12

MULTITASKING IS NOT A SUPERPOWER

I've been thinking about the last time I talked with my dad. Calling it a conversation would be a bit of an exaggeration. I would like to say it was a movie moment where he imparted some great life-altering wisdom like Forrest Gump's "life is like a box of chocolates. You never know what you're going to get." I did learn a lesson that day, but it had nothing to do with what was said.

During my childhood, my dad was a provider and punisher, but not much of a parent. His coworkers knew him better than I did. They called him Elvis because of his mutton-chop sideburns. I knew him as the guy you didn't want to make angry or you would end up singing the Elvis song "I'm all shook up." He was not much of a talker or hugger. There are monks who are chattier and germaphobes more affectionate than he was.

Now that I'm a dad of three boys, I know all that I missed out on—no goodnight kisses, bedtime stories, prayers, impromptu life lessons, or "I love you to the moon and back." I always felt like I had his name but not his heart.

In 1999, the last year of my dad's life, cancer ate away at his body, but it also softened his disposition. He was finally ready to be a dad; I was ready to be a son. But it was too late. He was often sedated because he was enduring the latter stages of the disease. One day when we were alone at the hospital, he was asleep while I was reading beside his bed. He suddenly woke up and looked over at me. He whispered, "This has been tough." Here was this golden opportunity to engage, maybe grab his hand and say a prayer . . . look into his eyes and tell him the fight was almost over . . . give him a hug and say, "I love you, Dad." Instead, I was distracted by a book on theology. I assumed there would be plenty more opportunities. I acknowledged his statement, but I did not seize the moment. Tragically, I never got another chance. He died without ever waking up again, and this experience still haunts me.

This lost opportunity has become one of my greatest regrets and a strong catalyst to being fully present. I learned that day that multitasking is not a superpower—being fully present is. Because of that experience, I try to not take for granted the moments I have with people. I like to say that kids want your gifts, but they need your presence. The gift of being fully present is powerful. Talking to an elderly neighbor, having a face-to-face conversation with your friend, or refusing to check social media while at dinner with family is a gift that can never be taken away. Yet how many of these invaluable moments do we miss because we are distracted?

Multitasking is not a superpower— being fully present is.

Many of us today resemble one of those one-man bands, who play a guitar with their hands, drums with their feet, cymbals with their knees, and a harmonica with their mouth. Unlike the street musician, we often sound more like noise than music. We surf the internet while watching TV. We text while we drive (no, Mom, not me). We post to Facebook while listening to a sermon. We check email while our family desperately tries to get our undivided attention. We think we are living life to the full, but we are living like a fool. God is the only being in the universe who can truly multitask. When we try to do it, we rob ourselves and others of our best. I saw a sign once that summed this up well: "Multitasking: the art of messing several things up at once."

The importance of being fully present was reinforced to me from an unlikely source. The book of Job seems like one of the most depressing books in the Bible. After Job tragically loses everyone and everything he cares about, he is stuck with three friends who just seem to make matters worse. Most of the book features a conversation between these friends as they wrestle with Job's pain and loss, wondering whether he deserves all the bad things that have happened to him. With friends like that who needs enemies? But Job's friends do one thing right: they sit with him in silence for seven days (see Job 2:11–13).

When I visit a person in the hospital, I'm typically there from fifteen minutes to an hour. I've never sat with someone for seven days. I don't think anyone could handle my sarcasm for that long.

A question people often ask about attending funerals is, "What do I say?" Often, the greatest gift you can offer is not your words. People may not remember what you say, but they will remember your presence.

> *Giving the gift of presence can be one of the most powerful and heroic things you can do.*

Lately, I've been memorizing James 1:27: "Religion that God our Father accepts as pure and faultless is this: to look after orphans and widows in their distress and to keep oneself from being polluted by the world." At the top of what God looks for is protecting and providing for orphans and widows.

As I thought about this, I started feeling convicted, because while I serve a few hundred people every weekend at church, it has been at least six months since I visited a very important widow in my life. My Aunt Leona is in her eighties. Physically, she could still take me in an arm-wrestling contest. Mentally, her mind is an Etch A Sketch. As soon as I leave the room, it's shaken and I'm forgotten.

During my recent visit, the question she kept asking me was, "Do you stop by often?" All I could say was, "Not as often as I should." She has no idea whether I stop by or not. My visiting earns me no credit with her. Heroes serve out of responsibility, not recognition.

In a culture where everyone is busy and preoccupied, giving the gift of presence can be one of the most powerful and heroic things you can do.

Chapter 13

COURAGE IS CONTAGIOUS

n the movie *Ant-Man*,[1] the first Ant-Man, Hank Pym, tells the future Ant-Man Scott Lang, that he must now step into the role of the insect-sized superhero. Lang responds: "One question. Is it too late to change the name?"

Most superheroes have a secret identity, but a superhero name strikes fear in the hearts of their enemies.

> Peter Parker is Spider-Man.
> Bruce Wayne is Batman.
> Jean Grey is Phoenix.
> Logan is Wolverine.
> T'Challa is Black Panther.

While we often think of comic characters as kid-friendly, they often take the form of animals and insects that typically give us the heebie-jeebies in real life. Who doesn't become an instant ninja when they walk into a spider web? Or run away screaming when a bat swoops down from the sky? These character names were originally meant to be scary.

Many warriors throughout history acquired intimidating names. Alexander the Great. Richard the Lionheart. Eric Bloodaxe. Their names make you want to surrender before the actual person even shows up. They often represent people of courage, victory, brutality, and relentlessness.

But I'm pretty sure no one ever said, "Do you know what name is tough? Jonathan." Maybe John, as in Robin Hood's Little John, John Cena, or my dad's favorite, John Wayne. But not Jonathan. However, the biblical Jonathan was a force to be reckoned with—not because of the size of his muscles but because of his God-sized courage.

Israel was getting bullied again by the Philistines, the same people that had given birth to the giant Goliath. Most of Israel's troops were hiding in caves and thickets with King Saul, even though they had the most powerful weapon on the planet, God. They had spiritual amnesia and once again had forgotten all the times God had come to their rescue (see 1 Sam. 12–13).

Fortunately, there was still at least one man who hadn't forgotten: Saul's son Jonathan. He refused to hide in caves and decided to go up against the Philistines himself. First Samuel 14:6 tells us that "Jonathan said to his young armor-bearer, 'Come, let's go over to the outpost of those uncircumcised men. Perhaps the LORD will act in our behalf. Nothing can hinder the LORD from saving, whether by many or by few.'" After waiting for the Lord's sign to advance, Jonathan and his young armor-bearer marched into battle. Perhaps the word *march* is misleading. They actually had to climb into battle, clawing their way up the side of a cliff.

Despite the fact that they were vastly outnumbered— there were twenty trained warriors waiting to treat Jonathan and his armor-bearer like piñatas—"the Philistines fell before Jonathan, and his armor-bearer followed and killed behind him" (1 Sam. 14:13). Then the entire Philistine army was struck by panic and fled.

Jonathan wasn't driven by military strategy. He wasn't following Sun Tzu's *The Art of War*. He was following God's lead, a heavenly Commander known for giving counterintuitive orders that defy human logic. Here are some other examples:

- The Lord instructed Joshua to have the army march around Jericho for seven days, asking him to trust that the walls would miraculously fall. (Josh. 6:2–5)
- God plucked Gideon out of obscurity to save Israel from the Midianites. Then he reduced Gideon's army from thousands to just three hundred men so it would be obvious who truly won the victory. (Judg. 6–7)
- To rescue the Israelites from slavery in Egypt, God instructed Moses to lead a few million citizens toward the open sea, with an angry army in hot pursuit. (Ex. 14:13–28)

Jonathan was confident, because he knew the God he served. After Jonathan won that battle, the rest of Israel was inspired to join in the fight. Courage is contagious.

In 1953, when the first two people stood on the summit of Mount Everest, they proved that it could be done. Now over four thousand people have seen the view from the top of the world.[2] These are people who might not have had the courage if someone hadn't blazed a trail. Sometimes the world just needs one or two brave individuals to go first.

In 1954, Roger Bannister proved that humans could run a four-minute mile.[3]

In 1945, Chuck Yeager proved that we could break the sound barrier in an aircraft.[4]

In 1961, Russian Yuri Gagarin proved that people could travel to space.[5]

In 2013, Diana Nyad proved that a person can successfully swim the one hundred miles from Cuba to Florida.[6]

Jonathan proved that two people plus God equals victory.

We don't have to go to the movies or watch the History Channel to find examples of inspiration and courage. If we pay attention, we will see examples of bravery all around us.

There's a young woman in my church who helps choreograph the dances on Sunday mornings. When you know her story, you can't help but get choked up every time she takes the stage. She should have died as an infant. Her biological mother abused drugs while she was in the womb. As a baby, she stopped breathing several times a day and developed multiple health complications as she grew older.

> *Sometimes the world just needs one or two brave individuals to go first.*

Fortunately, a gracious family took her in and gave her the meticulous care she needed. She was a fighter and her tiny body was determined to dance. When she was only seven years old, her adoptive mom overheard her singing "Can't Give Up Now" by Mary, Mary. Her fighter's spirit inspires all who know her, and when she dances now as a woman healed by the God she loves, all of heaven dances with her because she is a walking miracle.

Who is waiting for you to inspire them?

You may be the motivation someone else needs to leave the comfort of a chair and go take a summit for God!

Chapter 14

BETTER THAN X-RAY VISION

One of the things I hate most about winter is getting sick. I hate that it's the "season for sneezing." It's amazing how much damage a microscopic virus can do. Chills, fever, draining, puking, trembling, aching, all caused by an enemy so small that the naked eye can't see it. In 1347, the Black Death arrived in Europe, and over the next five years, it killed more than 20 million people—almost one-third of the continent's population. All this horror was caused by a microscopic bacillus that was transmitted through the air and the bite of a rat or flea.[1]

In the same way that a virus or bacteria can wreak havoc on the body, so can a small thought plague the mind. How often do we fall prey to toxic thoughts?

I will never find a godly husband or wife.

I will never break this cycle of addiction.

I will never get out of debt.

God hates me.

Nobody loves me.

Stinking thinking has ruined friends, families, companies, and churches. Toxic thoughts threatened to ruin the life of a prophet named of Elijah. Ministry had become misery. Serving had become suffering. Calling had become a prison sentence. Let's look at one of the lowest points in his life: "Elijah was afraid and ran for his life. When he came to Beersheba in Judah, he left his servant there, while he himself went a day's journey into the wilderness. He came to a broom bush, sat down under it and prayed that he might die" (1 Kings 19:3–4).

To understand why Elijah is so depressed, we need to understand a bit about his role as a prophet. When we hear the word *prophet*, we think of someone who predicts the future, a sort of human Magic 8 Ball who can tell us the winning lottery numbers or our chances of falling in love. One of the critical roles of the prophets was to communicate to the people on the Lord's behalf and to remind them of His commands and promises, warning them what would happen if they lived however they wanted rather than following the Lord's directions.

There's a story that has circulated for many years about how simple it is to trap a monkey. All you must do is put a banana in a monkey jar. The monkey will reach in, and when he closes his fist around it, he can't pull his hand back out. Because rather than let go, the monkey will continue to hold on, determined to retrieve the banana. It's on Wikipedia so it must be true.

Like monkeys hanging on to elusive bananas, we often grab hold of things like relationships, addictions, or hurts and refuse to let go even though it's enslaving us. We hold on in spite of the fact they cost us intimacy with God and integrity with others. We know we should let go, but stubbornly we hold on. It was the job of the prophet to point out when people had their hand stuck in the monkey jar. And this may surprise you, but people don't usually appreciate being told that they're wrong or that God is angry with them. In fact, people tend to get really angry, even violent. People defensively state "judge not lest you be judged."

And when Elijah went around telling people that they needed to stop worshiping the false god Baal, the situation escalated into a showdown between Elijah and the prophets of Baal. When I was a kid and things got heated between classmates, the threats would start with "I'm gonna beat you up after school" and end with "My dad is going to beat up your dad." To my knowledge, this threat was never carried out. Elijah challenged the prophets to set up an altar to their god and he would set up an altar to his God, then whichever god rained down fire from heaven was the true God. He was essentially claiming, "My God can beat up your god." And in a contest that is unprecedented and never repeated, the God of Israel ignited the altar like a "Holywood" pyrotechnics display while the prophets of Baal embarrassed themselves with loud prayers and dancing that were only met with silence.

The prophets were decisively beaten, and Queen Jezebel's "rent-a-god" was proven to be false. Jezebel then placed a bounty on Elijah's life—no idle threat since she had already systematically slaughtered several of the Jewish prophets. The probability of escape seemed slim to none. In addition to being put on the "hit list," Elijah thought he was the only one left who was fully devoted to God. He assumed there was no one else passionately pursuing Yahweh.

"'I have had enough, LORD,' he said. 'Take my life; I am no better than my ancestors.' Then he lay down under the bush and fell asleep" (1 Kings 19:4–5). When Elijah was plagued by the thoughts *I can't go on, I can't make a difference, I can't see hope on the horizon*, what he was really saying was, "I can't trust God to protect me," "I can't trust God to give me strength," "I can't trust God to use these difficult circumstances for my good and God's glory." His toxic thoughts were ruining his life, faith, hope, and peace, preventing him from moving forward with his mission.

Ironically, God had just flexed His miraculous muscles. He definitely answered Elijah's 58-word prayer to show up and say, "Ta-da, I'm real!" (see 1 Kings 18:36–37). I'm sure the apologist Ravi Zacharias would love to finish one of his debates with an atheist with God spontaneously setting an altar on fire. It's easy to argue with a philosophical position, but it's hard to argue with a powerful demonstration from heaven. I would love to have fire from heaven as an option when I'm telling my neighbors about Jesus.

You would think an experience like this would have given Elijah a sky-high confidence, and that he would never experience a day with doubt. But faith dissipates; our trust in God tends to be situational. *Sure God showed up then,* he may have thought, *but what guarantee do I have that He has my back this time? Sure God proved himself to the prophets of Baal, but can I trust Him to protect me from Queen Jezebel? Sure God is all powerful, but is God all love?*

When God asks Elijah what he is doing, he replies, "I have zealously served the Lord God Almighty. But the people of Israel have broken their covenant with you, torn down your altars, and killed every one of your prophets. I am the only one left, and now they are trying to kill me, too" (1 Kings 19:10 NLT).

There are two thoughts that cause Elijah to feel as if his situation is hopeless:

I'm the only one serving God.

Jezebel is going to kill me.

But it turns out both thoughts were dead wrong. God goes on to instruct Elijah in establishing leaders who will preserve His legacy and promises that there will be a remnant of seven thousand people in Israel who would continue serving Him (see 1 Kings 19:15–18). Elijah later becomes one of only two people in Scripture who escapes physical death altogether. His emotional tailspin was unwarranted. His toxic thoughts did not reflect reality. Elijah desperately needed God to tweak his perspective.

A young lady from my church who had been struggling with toxic thoughts most of her life, wrote the following words on Facebook:

"Instead of praying for a change of circumstances, pray for a change of perspective." Words spoken by Pastor Dan Stanford that changed my life. To say I struggled for my first 29 years would be putting it mildly. And then one day, after months of my brother asking me to go, I stepped into The Well [Church] for the first time. I was saved. I found my faith and was not afraid to declare it. I am no longer angry about all of the wrongs in my life. I am no longer hurt by all the pain. I am no longer sad from all the loss. Instead, I am constantly overwhelmed by all of God's blessings. My life is far from perfect. But I am thankful for every single second of it. Every single moment. I cannot even fully grasp the concept of Easter Sunday without tears streaming down my face. It's too much for my heart to take . . . I am so thankful.

Throughout life, we label our experiences, and depending how we interpret them determines how we respond emotionally, mentally, physically, and spiritually. Two people can hear about, witness, or go through the same experience but have totally different reactions because of their different perspectives. As the saying goes, "we do not see the world as it is but as we are."

As Christians, we have to filter our worldview through God's Word. We need to humbly realize how limited our education and experiences can be. God helps us label our experiences accurately, and sometimes He uses people of wisdom to do just that.

I want to share one more message from another young lady at my church:

> After a long day, I went to the pier and sat along the edge thinking some scary thoughts. I convinced myself to walk back to my car to be safe from my mind. I ended up seeing this girl, who seemed shaken up, walking toward the edge of the pier that I just left. I suddenly felt concerned for her so I followed her to the edge. I felt like I was meant to be there. She was swaying back and forth on the edge, when I grabbed her hand and pulled her back. I asked if she was all right and if she needed someone to talk to. We exchanged reasons as to why we were at the pier at this time of night, the issues we were currently dealing with, our past, and fears. We encouraged each other to push through these hardships. She admitted that if I didn't talk to her that moment, she would've commit suicide by jumping off the pier. She said I saved her life, but little did she know, she saved mine as well. God worked through me to save her. I've found another reason as to why I am here on earth.

Elijah overcame his toxic thinking by getting alone with God. He climbed up Mount Horeb and allowed God's thoughts to reshape his thoughts. Elijah was convinced that he was the only one left passionately pursuing God. This was proven false when God whispered that there were seven thousand people who had not turned their backs on Yahweh. Elijah

> *Sometimes our imagination needs to be challenged by revelation.*

was not alone. The situation wasn't as bad as he imagined. Elijah was a great prophet but a bad accountant. He crunched the numbers and only saw one when there were actually seven thousand and one.

Sometimes our imagination needs to be challenged by revelation. So many of life's crippling fears never become a reality. According to research conducted in 2015, 85 percent of what we worry about never becomes a reality.[2] In the same way, when we are haunted by our thoughts, we need God's perspective. This can come through a passage of Scripture or people of wisdom. We don't typically have to climb a mountain but we do need to create margin. It's hard to hear God's whispers on the go.

Chapter 15

THE ORIGINAL SUPERPOWER

Have you ever gotten a song stuck in your head and then had a hard time shaking it off? Many musicians try to imbed phrases and beats in their songs that hook you as you listen, and then stick with you. You might find yourself humming the same tune throughout the day. You become a walking radio station and free advertisement . . . unless you can't sing.

Like songs, other words and statements can get stuck in your head. A teacher once implied you were dumb, and you go through life feeling intellectually inferior. Someone in your high school called you fat, and you spend a lifetime trying to overcome your sense of insecurity. A relative asks why you can't be more like your older sibling, and you feel you have

> *Our words are powerful, and the things that are spoken into our lives have long-lasting ramifications.*

to constantly strive to prove yourself. Psychologists and professional counselors earn good money helping their clients identify the false statements that have defined their lives.

Our words are powerful, and the things that are spoken into our lives have long-lasting ramifications. As we learn in the book of James: "The tongue is a small part of the body, but it makes great boasts. Consider what a great forest is set on fire by a small spark. . . . With the tongue we praise our Lord and Father, and with it we curse human beings, who have been made in God's likeness" (James 3:5, 9).

Growing up, I never felt like I measured up physically. I heard all the "you're so skinny" jokes. While many people pray for the scale to go down, I prayed for it to go up. I drank chalky protein shakes, and unlike the before and after pictures, I still looked like the before guy, only bloated. I was often picked last during gym, because I was more of an artist than an athlete. At one point I was handcuffed to a school locker and whipped with a wet towel by a bully while other kids egged him on. It was not only the gravity of the insensitive words that weighed me down, it was also the overt message of the movies and magazines. If I wanted to be a man, then I needed a beard, biceps, and an ability to kill spiders without recoiling in fear.

Some of the hardest lessons at school don't take place in the classroom. One of those lessons is that the playground chant "sticks and stones may break my bones but words will never hurt me" is a pile of malarkey. All the kids who are cyberbullied can tearfully tell us about the battle wounds from the war of words. While a bone can heal within a month, words have a way of burrowing their way into our subconscious and haunting us for years. As an adult I was asked to play Jesus in a passion play. My biggest fear was that I would have to take off my shirt during the crucifixion scene. I was a grown man with a decent physique and yet I was still crippled by the scarring statements of kids from my childhood. Words don't have an expiration date. It's been said that time heals all wounds. But when it comes to verbal baggage, it's God's truth that heals all wounds.

I may be built more like Spider-Man than the Incredible Hulk, but God says that "I am fearfully and wonderfully made." The bathroom scale is not how I measure my value. Physical appearance is so unimportant that we are never given a description of what Jesus looked like. The gospel writers were more interested in His message and mission than in how long His hair was or how thick His build. We, too, should be more interested in character. God's Word has taken the sting out of the "you're so skinny" jokes.

God can use us to speak words of healing to others, as well as to speak wisdom.

Moses's father-in-law, Jethro, gave some critical advice to Moses after he led the Israelites out of Egypt. Moses was trying to lead two million people on his own, interpreting

God's will, and settling all their disputes. This was unsustainable, and Jethro saw that Moses needed to delegate: "What you are doing is not good. You and these people who come to you will only wear yourselves out. The work is too heavy for you; you cannot handle it alone" (Ex. 18:17–18). Jethro's advice to share the workload prevented Moses from getting burned out. Moses could have ignored his father-in-law, protesting that he had heard directly from God. But instead Moses humbly took the advice of his elder, and the whole nation benefitted as a result.

Before the advent of Google, most people asked their grandparents or other elders for advice. I think our generation can easily neglect this. It is a great privilege and gift to humbly listen to those with more life experience. They might just share a powerful insight or encouragement that we need to succeed like Jethro shared with Moses.

Words are powerful. Have you ever fallen asleep while reading the Bible? Maybe you were reading through the book of Leviticus, which can be more potent than a sedative. Or maybe you started to snooze as you skimmed through one of the family-tree sections reading names like Amram, Izhar, and Uzziel. A few years ago, I was reading the Bible when I kept falling asleep. Exhausted, I dropped my Bible over the side of the bed. The next morning, I woke up and discovered that I had killed a mouse with God's Word. Can you believe the timing of that? This little mouse happened to be running across the room at the same time I dropped my Bible. I could tell it had been running, because it looked like an Olympic sprinter, caught mid-stride. Talk about powerful.

Long before I "smote" that poor mouse with my Bible, God used His words to bring the universe into existence. God said, "Let there be light" (Gen. 1:3), and the moment His voice rang out, radiant light flooded the sky, pushing back the darkness. How intense is that? God said, "Let the land produce vegetation" (Gen. 1:11), and instantly trees, bushes, plants, and flowers exploded into life across the earth, creating magnificent textures, colors, and smells. God said, "Let the land produce living creatures" (Gen. 1:24), and giraffes, elephants, porcupines, and hyenas began roaming the planet.

God could have used a host of methods to create life, but He chose to use His words. I believe God wanted to establish from the very beginning that His words are powerful. Paul sums this up with the instruction to "be transformed by the renewing of your mind" (Rom. 12:2). The word translated here as transformed is *morpho*, the same word used for an embryo growing in its mother's womb. God's Word has the capability to help us grow, change our perspective, and reset our attitude. By meditating on and applying God's Word to our lives, we morph into the men and women God created us to be.

A handful of Marvel and DC characters use their voice as a weapon. Characters like the Black Canary or the Silver Banshee use sound waves to fly, immobilize people, and destroy structures. Since we are created in God's image, our words have the potential to be powerful as well. While we can't create worlds with our words, we can shape attitudes, actions, values, and beliefs.

As a father I can't imagine anything more powerful than

Horatio Spafford writing the words, "It is well with my soul" as he traveled over the spot where his four daughters had drowned.[1] How many struggling, grieving people have sung those words and found comfort?

Or how about when Martin Luther was on trial for his Reformation writings and courageously said, "My conscience is captive to the Word of God. Thus I cannot and will not recant, because acting against one's conscience is neither safe nor sound."[2]

Or how about the apostle Paul who is sitting in a first-century jail without the guarantee of "three hots and a cot," yet writes, "Rejoice in the Lord always. I will say it again: Rejoice!" (Phil. 4:4).

Lyrics can inspire us to worship or to dance. Speeches can motivate us to act. Jokes can make us laugh. Twitter messages can anger us. Books can change our opinions. Screenplays can move us to tears. Words shape worlds.

When I first accepted Christ, my inner world looked like a postapocalyptic disaster movie. Attributes like love, joy, and peace had crumbled, like skyscrapers after a nuclear fallout, under years of self-inflicted abuse. My self-esteem might as well have been ravaged by zombies. There was life, but it was tainted with death and doubt.

Jesus had moved in, but all the lies that had shaped my life had yet to move out. I had accepted the embodiment of truth and life, but it was a seed that needed to slowly take root, germinate, and overtake my inner world. God would strategically use mentors who nurtured my seedling faith with words of healing and hope.

A grandmother told me about all of the apostle Paul's sins and that there was nothing I could have done as a teenager that was unforgivable. If God could forgive me, how dare I refuse to forgive myself? Was I better than God? (Man, I love the bluntness of a seasoned saint.)

There was a youth pastor who challenged me to grow some spiritual backbone. "You walk around hunched over like Quasimodo beating yourself up. You have to stop allowing your past to define you. Embrace who Christ says you are. You're loved. You're forgiven. You're free."

Then a couple gave me my first opportunity to preach, even though I saw myself behind the scenes, a part of the support staff running the sound, cleaning the bathrooms, and greeting people on their way in (washing my hands first, of course). But that couple saw someone called by God to share His words.

It has been ordinary people that God has used to reshape my inner world by their words. What once looked like a post-battle scene from Hulk vs. Doomsday now looks more like a garden producing the fruit of love, joy, and peace.

James wrote, "If you claim to be religious but don't control your tongue, you are fooling yourself, and your religion is worthless" (James 1:26 NLT). If James were alive today, he would probably say, "So what if you never miss a Sunday service and you can quote the book of Lamentations, if you routinely use your words to tell dirty jokes, lie to your spouse, talk bad about your boss, verbally abuse your kids, or throw a 'mantrum' (when a grown man throws a tantrum)."

Many relationships unravel because of careless conversations. A fascinating study was conducted on seven hundred couples that had just received their marriage licenses. Each couple was videotaped having a fifteen-minute conversation, and based on the amount of negative and positive comments they exchanged, the researchers were able to predict with a 97 percent accuracy which couples would end in divorce. According to their research, the magic ratio is five to one. A person needs to hear five positives for every one negative thought to maintain optimal emotional health.[3]

My wife and I were washing the dishes when I said to her, "I was watching the news the other day. They just discovered a mountain bigger than Mt. Everest." Shocked she said, "Really?" At that point I delivered the punch line. "Yeah, it's in our bedroom, and it's made out of dirty laundry." Guess who had to finish the dishes alone and take care of the laundry? Words have weight. What we say can be constructive or destructive.

We worship God on Sunday and insult His kids the rest of the week. Yet how many of us would be best friends with someone who routinely cussed at and cut down our kids? How can we expect to stay in God's favor when we verbally abuse His children?

Once a word leaves our mouth, we lose control over it. We can't erase it, delete it, or white it out. There are no takebacks. You can apologize, but you can never fully undo the damage. We don't know how far it will travel and what degree of impact it is going to have. Words are like a child in that, once they are born, they take on a life of their own. Therefore, James challenges us to be slow to speak. To take advantage of the fact that we are not mind readers, we can choose what thoughts we are willing to relinquish control over.

Words are powerful. I preached my first sermon a few weeks after encountering Jesus. Without any seminary training, I sat down and began to write. Ten pages poured out of me. I sent them to a half dozen friends and family. I risked rejection and ridicule but couldn't live with myself if I played it safe. The only thing worse than failure is living with the regret of *what if*? A few of the friends who received that letter embraced Jesus and are still an active member in church twenty years later.

I love using words to serve God and others. I have been consistently surprised and humbled when a person says that they experienced hope or healing through the words that I have shared. I know that, on my own, my words would be as powerless as Superman around kryptonite. At the end of Peter's first sermon in the book of Acts, it says that the people "were cut to the heart" (Acts 2:37). This wasn't because of Peter's verbal skills but because of the power of the Holy Spirit working through him.

Friedrich Nietzsche once said, "All I need is a sheet of paper and something to write with, and then I can turn the world upside down."[4] We are often surrounded by people who have been wounded by words, whose worlds are topsy-turvy. They desperately need us to come save the day with a thoughtful text, tweet, or handwritten note.

Is there someone in your life who would benefit from your superpower to encourage or challenge?

Chapter 16

THE POWER OF PERSEVERANCE

What is the longest distance you have ever run? I remember the first time I ran the mile as an adult. As my lungs were burning and my side was cramping, I kept thinking, *Why would a person do this unless they were being chased by a bear or a band of ninjas?* In spite of my body's protests, I was running with a friend during the summer. We were training for our second Tough Mudder. The Tough Mudder is a twelve-mile race with twenty-five, military-grade obstacles throughout the course that incorporate electrocution, subzero temperatures, and many other hair-raising challenges.

After six miles of running through the woods and mud,

he told me, "I know the perfect spot to stop. There's this little hill." The word *hill* is misleading. The Black Hills reach seven thousand feet in elevation.[1] We started climbing, and every five steps I felt ten years older. I couldn't breathe. I was making noises I'd never heard before. I looked up at my friend, who was already nearing the top. I had a talk with God. "How is it that You not only gave him strength (the dude could play the Incredible Hulk's stunt double), but You also felt it necessary to give him speed and stamina? Speed should be my thing." Despite my jealousy, I was motivated as I saw him crest the hilltop. There was no way I was letting him stand on the summit without me.

Perseverance is inspiring. I'm willing to bet that all of us can point to at least one person whose dogged refusal to give up has renewed our hope, our hunger, and our desire to ascend. In the same way, there are others who are waiting for you to inspire them.

Every hero faces a moment in the race of life that makes them second guess if they have what it takes to move forward.

Bruce Banner doesn't know if he can manage his anger.

Black Widow doesn't know if she can let go of her past.

Iron Man is not sure he can overcome his panic attacks.

It's one thing to live and lead from a place of wholeness, but none of us have that luxury. We have to rise to the occasion in spite of pasts, pains, and personal problems.

Fun runs, obstacle races, and even half and full marathons are becoming more and more popular with an estimated 17.1 million Americans finishing in such events in 2015.[2] While there are a lot of mud runs and marathons, the longest race, and often the most grueling, is the race of life. Listen to how the author of Hebrews puts it:

> Therefore, since we are surrounded by such a great cloud of witnesses, let us throw off everything that hinders and the sin that so easily entangles. And let us run with perseverance the race marked out for us, fixing our eyes on Jesus, the pioneer and perfecter of faith. For the joy set before him he endured the cross, scorning its shame, and sat down at the right hand of the throne of God. (Heb. 12:1–2)

The author of Hebrews gives us some inspiration for putting one foot in front of the other when we desperately need a second wind. In most races, there's some type of prize, cash, trophy, T-shirt and bragging rights. When I finished the Tough Mudder, I got a sweatband. Who even wears sweatbands any more besides Richard Simmons? In the ancient Greek games, a victor was crowned with a garland or wreath.[3] As runners came down the final stretch, they were exhausted, perhaps in agony, and feeling as though they couldn't go another step. But suddenly there was the prize in sight, and a new burst of energy would kick in.

A part of the race that was set before Jesus was the excruciating pain of dying on the cross, enduring humiliation, torture, and a slow, agonizing death. The author states that Jesus was motivated to endure the cross because of the "joy set before him" (Heb. 12:2). Jesus looked beyond the cross to what would be accomplished through the cross.

> *Jesus looked beyond the cross to what would be accomplished through the cross.*

Jesus saw you and me, and love motivated Him to keep running. When exhausted, we need to imagine who is waiting on the other side. Who will benefit from our endurance and perseverance?

By beginning this series of verses with the word *therefore*, the author points back to the end of the previous chapter 11, where he listed several people who won the race of life despite the unique challenges each of them had to face. What does it mean to win the race of life in God's eyes?

Noah faced the flood, built an ark, and witnessed God's faithfulness.

Rahab hosted two servants of God at the risk of her family's safety and watched God miraculously protect her home as the rest of the city crumbled around her.

Moses faced over a million complaining people and watched God provide and protect despite the miles of desert and months of disobedience.

Daniel faced a den of hungry lions and walked out with all his digits and an inspiring story.

Hannah faced infertility, prayed for a miracle, and gave birth to one of Israel's greatest prophets, Samuel.

One of my favorite examples of God's love and power is the story of an unnamed prophet in 2 Kings 6 who faced the possibility of embarrassment and debt, but instead experienced an unusual miracle. A group of prophets were working on a construction project. If they are anything like me, they were better with their words than their hands! So it probably wasn't a surprise when one of the guys dropped his axe in the Jordan River. He started to freak out but strategically ran to get Elisha. The situation is not a matter of life and death but it is life and debt since he had borrowed the axe. And he can't just run to a hardware store. Elisha's knee-jerk reaction was to pray rather than panic, and he made the heavy metal object defy the laws of physics and float. It's as if a pocket of zero gravity surrounded it. (It would be great to have this miracle available just before your cellphone drops into the toilet.)

When the axe floated, hope floated as well. This story is a perfect example of the promise, "Cast your cares on the LORD and he will sustain you" (Ps. 55:22). Whatever obstacle is in your way, God can help you hurdle it.

When I read through Hebrews chapter 11, I imagine a stadium full of people who have already finished life's race, and are cheering us on from heaven. They are shouting, "You can do it!" The reason the author includes this chapter is that the perseverance of others is motivating. I was reminded of this when I participated in my first Tough Mudder. What kept me going was my friend and teammate Tony who has MS but refused to let it slow him down. Weeks before we competed in the race, he actually had one eye that would randomly go blind. His legs would become numb and give out. He had every excuse to slack off, and yet he pressed through every hill, every challenge. It was inspiring. There was no way I was going to let him cross the finish line alone.

During the Tough Mudder there's a climactic obstacle called Everest, which you encounter near the end of the race. It's a fifteen-foot half-pipe caked in mud and blood. Even Spider-Man would have a hard time scaling this beast. The goal is to run as fast as you can with your already cramped calves and leap, arms and body outstretched, ignoring the potential to miss the grab and go tumbling back down. You hope that you get enough momentum to reach the top the first time because you don't have enough gas in the tank for a second try. Tony was determined to conquer Everest. The most emotional moment was when he locked eyes with us, signaling that he was expecting us, who were already at the top, to catch him. He bolted forward, face grimacing, muscles exploding, every step determined and desperate. He threw himself skyward and as a team we caught him by his fingers and hoisted him up. At least that's how I think it happened, my eyes may have been a little blurry because of the mud and tears. I was so proud of him.

In the Tough Mudder it is an unspoken rule that you can bypass any of the obstacles. But Tony insisted on conquering every one of them in spite of having every excuse to take the easier route. His endurance was electrifying. It was literally electrifying since he got zapped so many times by the obstacles with 10,000 volts of DC electricity, which is enough to resurrect Frankenstein's monster. You can become someone else's hero just by putting one foot in front of the other.

Not giving up on a difficult marriage.

Not giving up on a difficult teenager or toddler.

Not giving up on a difficult boss or job.

Not giving up on a frustrating church.

Will you prevail or bail? Will you drop out or go all out? Will you quit or be too legit to quit?

We had a guest speaker at our church once who fainted halfway through her message. Our stage is a few feet tall, and she started tumbling headfirst toward the floor. Fortunately, I was seated close enough that I could spring forward and catch her. In that moment, I was thankful she wasn't our family pastor, because he's twice my size. I would have looked like the Wicked Witch of the East after Dorothy's house dropped on her. The guest speaker woke up quickly, confused as to what had happened. A doctor and nurse in the congregation checked her out right away. After it was determined that her nerves had most likely caused her blood pressure to drop, she insisted on finishing the talk.

While many people would have taken the out, she wanted to finish what she started and did a masterful job. It reminded me of a story Pastor John Ortberg told about one of the first times he preached and he passed out. The next week the congregation heard about his fainting and the attendance grew. Everyone wanted to know if it was going to happen again.[4] It's not the ideal way to create church growth, but you use what you can. While the young lady at my church gave a motivating message, her perseverance was the lesson most people took home that day.

It is likely that you will have one of these moments where you must give up or step up. Will you heroically put one foot in front of the other?

Chapter 17

SEEING
THE INVISIBLE

Most of us are familiar with the "selfie" and probably a lot of us frequently share our selfies with friends and family. There are some famous selfies now. One of my favorites is an astronaut hovering in space with the earth for a backdrop. Social media exploded when Pope Francis posed for a selfie with a few of his religious fans. There are thousands of selfies of people flexing their biceps in the mirror. There's even a T-shirt that says "I train for the selfies." Many people don't seem to realize that they can go to the gym without posting pictures online and still burn calories.

The French philosopher Descartes once said, "I think therefore I am."[1] There is a segment of culture that seems to say, "I selfie therefore I am." You can't scroll through social media without bumping into one of these self-made portraits. In 2015, Kim Kardashian published a book titled *Selfish*. It's nearly four hundred fifty pages of the reality star's pictures of herself. She is not alone in this trend. One in four Americans regularly post selfies on social media, and that number is growing.[2] Over 50 percent of millennials post selfies regularly,[3] and according to the company Samsung, the average American will post over 25,000 selfies in their lifetime.[4]

Actor James Franco, who has been called "the king of the selfie," says, "In our age of social networking, the selfie is the new way to look someone right in the eye and say, 'Hello, this is me.'"[5] As human beings, we want to be seen. Toddlers ask family to watch them jump off the couch or spin in a circle. Teenagers post videos of themselves and ask their peers if they are ugly or cute. Guys wear sleeveless T-shirts that say, "Sun's out, guns out." We post pictures on Facebook, Twitter, and Instagram hoping for enough comments, likes, and positive emojis. For many of us, to be looked at is to be loved. If a picture is worth a thousand words, then a selfie seems to be summed up in three: "look at me."

Though over a million selfies are taken and shared every day, many people still feel invisible. We can walk into a room and go mostly unnoticed. We sometimes wonder if anyone would pay attention if we left the company, transferred schools, or dropped out of our local church. There's no paparazzi chasing us around trying to capture meaningful moments from our life. No one is standing in line trying to get our autograph or phone number. Maybe we feel overlooked because we're getting older and we live in a culture obsessed with youth. It's assumed that once a person reaches sixty-five they will retire, take a backseat, and go on a permanent vacation. The elderly are not seen as an important part of companies, culture, or the church. Long before relatives stop going to see them at the retirement home, they already feel forgotten.

Some of us feel invisible because our spouse doesn't seem to notice us anymore. We can get a new haircut or outfit, but they are oblivious. We're pretty sure they would notice a missing one hundred dollars before they would notice if we were missing. We feel like we get more face-to-face time with the local barista than we do with the one with whom we exchanged vows to love and cherish.

In the Song of Solomon, we read about a man who went out of his way to make his spouse feel seen. Forty times over eight chapters, he paints a word picture of how beautiful she is. He writes things like, "Your teeth are white like newly sheared sheep just coming from their bath. Each one has a twin, and none of them is missing" (Song 4:2 NCV). This is not a typical pickup line, but I imagine there are some parts of the world where having all your teeth would be a big deal. Many an emotional or physical affair started because a spouse was paid attention while feeling ignored at home. "Have you lost weight?" "Those jeans look great on you!" "Has anyone ever told you how cute your dimples are when you smile?" Seeing and spotlighting the positive attributes of our spouse is a powerful thing.

In junior high, I hit an awkward phase. I was skinny, shy, and not very athletic. My imagination was rich, but my relationships were poor. I often sat alone at lunch. One day, a guy started talking to me. I was so starved for attention, I jumped at the friendship. After chatting for a few minutes, he asked for my number so we could hang out later. I discovered the next day that he carved the digits into the table with the added message, "for a good time call Dan." I don't know what hurt more, his betrayal or the fact that no one called.

Listen to the tear-jerking words of David: "my father and mother forsake me" (Ps. 27:10). While David means this figuratively and uses it to contrast his confidence in the presence of God, many people have literally been or feel abandoned by those who should love them most. Contrast this idea with Moses's parents, who by faith "hid him for three months after he was born, because they saw he was no ordinary child" (Heb. 11:23). Some parents look at their child, and all they can see is responsibility. Empowering and loving parents consider their son or daughter and see ability.

For example, Malala is the youngest Nobel Peace Prize winner to date. She won at the age of sixteen, but her prize came at a great cost. She grew up in Pakistan. Because of the Taliban, many Afghan girls are without education. Two hundred schools for girls have been detonated. The idea is that girls should take care of the home and give birth to babies, preferably boy babies. From a young age, Malala wanted to climb above this stereotype. In a culture where girls are often overlooked, her dad believed in her. He saw her as just as valuable as any son. He wanted her to get educated and to chase her dreams. They resisted the Taliban.

She continued to go to school despite threats. At the age of fourteen, she was on a bus when a young man walked on asking for her by name. Once she was identified, he shot her point blank in the head. Miraculously, she survived. Her story amazed us all, and now she travels around the world advocating for education and equality for women. She believes in the potential of young girls just like her dad believed in her. The quote on her website sums up her philosophy: "One child, one teacher, one book and pen can change the world."[6]

I recently read *Wonder* by R. J. Palacio, which is the story of a fifth-grade boy named August who has congenital facial defects. We watch his heart break as people isolate him, turn their eyes away, shrink back at his touch, and whisper when they think he doesn't notice. At one point, August says, "I think there should be a rule that everyone in the world should get a standing ovation at least once in their lives."[7] How much healthier would people's sense of worth be if everyone was guaranteed a life of feeling significant and seen? Few experience the thrill of being valedictorian, sitting in the corner office, making the game-winning catch, or creating a YouTube channel with over a million views. Some people feel like extras in the movie of life. Every society has people who feel invisible.

There's an inner-city church in Minnesota that has the world's greatest worship team. You have probably never heard of them and they will probably never release a worship album. I discovered them when I lived in Minneapolis. The church transformed their basement into a homeless shelter. Half the congregation is made up of recovering drug addicts, ex-gang members, and homeless people. When it was time for worship, the director invited the choir onto the stage. Half of the congregation walked to the front. When they began to sing, it was obvious that most of them had never had a voice lesson and were most likely tone deaf. Technically they were awful; spiritually they were incredible.

I have heard many worship teams that have sounded way better, but when this group worshiped, all of heaven smiled. They knew what amazing grace meant, and they let God know how much they appreciated it. I imagine if Jesus had to pick somewhere to attend on Sunday morning, this church would be one of His top choices. They may never break through the church growth barriers, but they are breaking through the barriers of racism, addiction, and hopelessness. The very people who society tends to overlook have hope because they know that God sees them.

One of the things I loved about this community is that they are guided by love, not labels. There were no holy hurdles that you had to jump through before you were embraced as a part of the community. It didn't matter if you hadn't showered for a week, you were still getting a hug. They didn't just put on the church sign, "all are welcome," they lived it. Church wasn't like going to a movie where we all sit next to each other watching the same experience but not really doing life together. Rather, this church felt like a family—a messy, beautiful family.

I think the reason things are different there is that grace is fresh for so many of the congregation. They know how dark life can be without Jesus. They know what it is like to be overlooked by society. Some of them have been abandoned by friends and family. They know what it is like to have people avert their eyes when passing them on the street. We need to feel seen. Once they felt seen by Jesus, they wanted everyone who came through the doors of the church to experience that same gift.

Jesus constantly broke down barriers. He slowed down long enough to consider the unseen. Eight times in the New Testament we read about Jesus going to dinner with someone. Five of those times were with someone who was considered socially unacceptable.[8] Sometimes the greatest gift we can give someone is to see them. Heroes see the invisible.

> *Sometimes the greatest gift we can give someone is to see them. Heroes see the invisible.*

Let me give a few examples. At my church, I try to mingle with all age groups. I pop in on the youth group and kids ministry. One night I noticed a teen playing Hacky Sack by himself while all the other teens were huddled in distinct groups. I made it a point to go over and play with him. This was not easy because I was wearing skinny jeans and my forty-year-old joints are not as flexible as they used to be. But he lit up when I offered to play, and then I invited others to join us. I saw him, and I invited others to see him. All of us have people in our life who feel unseen. Look for them. Put down the tablets and the phones. Refuse to avert your eyes; truly look at them.

One of the things I love about God is that there's never been a moment He's missed out on in my life. He's always fully present; He sees my every move—good, bad, or uncoordinated. He doesn't blink. He doesn't nap. He never looks away. As a dad I hate missing out on even one moment of my kids' lives. They probably are okay with that. They don't want me volunteering to chaperone the school dances. They don't want me go on their first date. They appreciate the fact that I'm not omnipresent. But missing out on the miraculous and mundane makes me sad.

Fortunately for all of us, even when we feel overlooked by society, God sees us. One of my favorite names for God is El Roi, which means "You are the God who sees me" (Gen. 16:13).

Have you ever had a nickname? Are you embarrassed by that name? Not everyone is fortunate enough to end up with something cool like the Rock or the Great Bambino. I not only had a nickname as a teenager, but I got it permanently tattooed on my leg. It was a dumb name, and I instantly regretted it. As somebody once said, "Everything happens for a reason." Sometimes that reason is that we are stupid and make bad decisions. Nicknames are often a reflection of our character or competence—bad or good. They say something about our identity.

God has several descriptive names that we can loosely consider "nicknames," including:

Alpha and Omega
Lion of Judah

Ancient of Days
King of Kings
Prince of Peace
Everlasting Father
Rock of Salvation
Refiner's Fire
Abba Father[9]

Only one person in Scripture had the opportunity to give a name to God—Yahweh always named Himself. But a slave woman named Hagar called God "El Roi," because God saw her when no one else did. In order to grasp the significance of this moment, you need to know a little bit about her story. Abram and Sarai had been married for a long time, but Sarai hadn't been able to get pregnant. So she came up with a desperate plan. She told Abram, "The LORD has kept me from having children. Go, sleep with my slave; perhaps I can build a family through her" (Gen. 16:2). Abram agreed to do this, and Sarai gave him Hagar as his second wife. At that time, finding a surrogate was not unusual since having children was the key to security in old age. Sarai probably felt like she was making the only sensible choice, even though she was taking control instead of taking God at His word.

Abram married Hagar, and she got pregnant. When Sarai and Hagar began to experience mutual enmity and strife, Sarai blamed the situation on her husband. Abram chose to remain passive and told her: "'Your slave is in your hands. . . . Do with her whatever you think best.' Then Sarai mistreated Hagar; so she fled from her" (Gen. 16:6). Hagar ran away to escape the abuse. She probably traveled about seventy miles, which would have taken a week on foot. She was pregnant. We don't know whether she had food or water, but she was alone and vulnerable to the weather, wild animals, and bandits. Slaves had no rights and were often treated like property. Even as Abram's second wife, her status hadn't changed much. In her moment of desperation, God showed up.

When we feel invisible, God sees us. God sees your warts and all and loves you. By the same token, one of the greatest gifts we can give others is to see them—to refuse to multitask or be distracted, to choose to be fully in the moment, to look in their eyes, to sit next to the person everyone else avoids. Your attention can be one of the greatest gifts in someone else's life.

While many of the Marvel and DC superheroes wear a disguise to protect their identity and are content to serve from the shadows, Tony Stark takes a different route. At the end of the wildly successful movie *Iron Man*, the billionaire is holding a press conference. Tony addresses the room of reporters and cameras, saying, "It is one thing to question the official story, and another thing entirely to make wild accusations, or insinuate that I'm a superhero." The reporter shoots back, "I never said you are a superhero." Tony says, "You didn't? . . . Well, good, because that would be outlandish and, uh, fantastic. I'm just not the hero type. Clearly. With this laundry list of character defects, all the mistakes I've made, largely public. . . . The truth is . . . I am Iron Man." Tony obviously has something of an ego and wants people to know that he was the one saving the day.[10] Like

Tony, our fantasies of doing something great are often driven by a desire to be seen.

I remember the first time I went to Willow Creek, a megachurch with about twenty-six thousand members. I had the chance to stand on the stage and look out at the seats. Someone asked me, "Can you ever imagine yourself preaching on this stage or preaching to this many people?" It seemed like such a "duh" question. "Of course I can," I shot back. I thought, *I'm destined for greatness.* I think every young preacher imagines a day when he will preach to a packed house. But not everyone has been called to be the next Billy Graham. Success in the kingdom is not measured by how large of a crowd you get to preach to or how publicly you get to exercise your gifts. We have all been called to live in such a way that we'll hear God say, "Well done, good and faithful servant" (Matt. 25:23). Not well done good *and famous* servant.

Whose approval and applause are you living for? Do you serve and share in order to get the attention of others? Jesus challenged some of the religious people of His day because they lived for the standing ovation of others. They prayed publicly for the spiritual street credit. Jesus challenged them to recalibrate their motives. Pray to bless God and not impress others. "And when you pray, do not be like the hypocrites, for they love to pray standing in the synagogues and on the street corners to be seen by others. Truly I tell you, they have received their reward in full. But when you pray, go into your room, close the door and pray to your Father, who is unseen. Then your Father, who sees what is done in secret, will reward you" (Matt. 6:5–6).

As I mentioned previously, I was a janitor for a time during college. One day while I was cleaning some pipes tucked under a sink, an employee walked into the bathroom. "Why are you cleaning those pipes? No one is ever going to see them."

I refrained from pointing out that he had seen them and simply said, "If you want to excel, practice excellence."

"Is that a company mantra?" he asked me.

"Nope. It's mine. The CEO may never see these pipes, but God does."

When you live only for God's approval, you're willing to serve in the shadows. You might enjoy the encouragement and recognition of others, but you don't need it because you know your significance comes from God.

Chapter 18

BECOMING A POWERFUL SYMBOL

I went to Chicago's Comic Con in 2017. I jokingly told my wife that it was called Comic Con because they kept trying to "con" me out of money. Four dollars for a bottle of water. A hundred and twenty-five dollars for a picture with a B-level actor or actress. Fifty dollars for a Gotham City police badge. The price of the badge would have been worth it if I could have arrested vendors for inflated prices.

Since I don't have the budget of billionaire Bruce Wayne, I avoided most of the them. I quickly discovered, though, that you don't have to spend money to have a blast because of the cosplay, a merging of the words *costume* and *play*. Men and women, both young and old, invest hard-earned money and time designing their own superhero costumes (not all of them appropriate) and wear them to events like this.

The cosplayers I met were very generous, often standing around for long periods of time taking pictures with fans of their costumes and/or the characters they were impersonating. Keep in mind these are not paid actors, just people who love comic book culture. There were several people dressed as the iconic Superman and Batman. The symbols and paraphernalia of these two DC superstars were everywhere you looked.

You don't have to be a superhero fan to recognize the S on Superman's chest or Batman's bat emblem. These symbols have saturated our culture for decades, since the debut of these characters in the late '30s. Their symbols transcend the generations, adored by eight-year-olds and eighty-year-olds alike. I saw these symbols on T-shirts, tattoos, and car decals. It's fascinating to me that we can see a red S or a black bat emblem and immediately make the connection. Symbols can be beautiful and powerful.

There's a scene in the movie *Man of Steel* when Lois Lane asks Superman what the S on his chest means. The Kryptonian explains, "It's not an S. On my world it means hope." Sarcastically she responds that on earth it's just an S.[1] While Lois is dismissive at first, it doesn't take long for her to see the why behind this symbol when Superman saves the planet from General Zod. The S will become a reminder that as long as the son of Jor-El is around, there is someone to save the day.

In the fictional city of Gotham, the bat emblem served as a symbol of hope as well. Whenever Commissioner Gordon flashed that symbol into the night sky, it didn't matter what villain the city was facing, everyone knew that the dynamic duo was going to swing in and save the day. When Adam West, one of the more iconic actors to play Batman, died in 2017, the bat signal was projected onto LA's City Hall. It was an emotional moment for the thousands of Batman fans gathered to pay tribute. It was painful to realize that Adam West would no longer slide down the pole into the Bat Cave, transforming from Bruce Wayne into Batman, jumping into the Batmobile, and going to Gotham's rescue.

We live in a world desperate for hope. As I wrote this chapter, Hurricane Harvey slammed into Houston, causing extensive flooding and killing over eighty people; Hurricane Irma caused extensive damage in the Caribbean and Florida and took the lives of more than sixty people; a powerful earthquake hit Mexico taking over three hundred lives; Hurricane Maria crashed into Puerto Rico, resulting in massive damage to homes, roads, and infrastructure and causing seventeen deaths; forest fires raged through California and the Pacific Northwest; and North Korea's leader Kim Jong-un repeatedly threatened nuclear war. Many days it seemed we should adopt the sign over Dante's Inferno, "All hope abandon, ye who enter here."

The world desperately needs a symbol of hope more powerful than the S on Superman's chest and the bat emblem that hovers over Gotham. During the first through fourth centuries, Christians used a lot of symbols to communicate with one another.[2] They used symbols like the fish, the cross, and the anchor. Symbols were an important

> *Jesus was the hero who saved not only the day but eternity.*

way to communicate concepts and messages since a high percentage of people at the time could not read or write.[3] One of the earliest symbols was the fish or *ichthus*.[4] Archaeologists have found hundreds of them in their excavations of tombs, catacombs, and buildings. The Greek spelling of the word comprises five letters, which in English stand for "Jesus Christ God's Son Savior."[5]According to some Bible scholars, this symbol may have been used as a coded reference for Jesus.[6]

The ichthus, cross, and anchor were all symbols of hope, visual reminders that Jesus was the hero who already saved not only the day but eternity. Even though first-century Christians lived at a time when they faced prison, loss of homes, friends, and family if their faith was discovered, Jesus was their ultimate provision and protection. They knew that their security was not based on the economy, military, or judicial system. Their security was in Jesus, who does not need a cape or catchphrase.

Hope for me is realizing that our prayer, "Your will be done, on earth as it is in heaven" (Matt. 6:10), will be realized. One day planet earth will experience the perfection of heaven. Marvel and DC superheroes can save the fictional world from the villain; but in the real world, only our Savior can rescue us from true evil. Only Jesus can usher in a day when heroes will no longer be needed because sin and pain and death will no longer be present.

My dad died in his early forties. It bothers me that he never got to see any of my kids. He never got to walk my sister down the aisle. He never got to hear one of my sermons. It bothers me that I never got to love on the baby we lost. It bothers me that there are terrorists who torture people for years before publicly executing them. It bothers me that people keep taking their despair out through mass shootings.

But my hope comes from believing that one day God will win, love will prevail, sickness will be cured, families will be reunited, and wrongs will be reversed.

Our tendency as humans is to forget the times God helped us in the past. We suffer from spiritual amnesia. Our faith becomes situational. We trust Him with our soul but not our finances. We trust Him with our forever but not our kids. We trust Him with our past but not our addictions. We forget that the God who came to our rescue so many times before can do so again now.

Instead, we can become symbols of hope when we practically lean into God during times of hardship and heartache and when we share the story of what God has done on our behalf. We bring hope when we remind people that someday God's kingdom will prevail. As it says in Romans 15:4, "For everything that was written in the past was written to teach us, so that through the endurance taught in the Scriptures and the encouragement they provide we might have hope."

Scripture is a résumé of God's faithfulness. When we read

about God providing for His people, it inspires hope in us. If God could rescue Noah from a flood, Daniel from a lion's den, David from a giant, and Deborah from an army, God can intervene in our situation as well. If God did it before, He will be faithful to do it again. These stories spur us on today. In the same way the lives of Bible characters inspire us to hope, we can inspire others to hope. As citizens of God's kingdom, we get to foreshadow what life in eternity will look like. We get to show the world what true love, joy, peace, and patience should be.

It's important not only to discover people in history you can look up to and emulate, but also to find people you know personally and call a friend. My wife, Suzanne, keeps me grounded and centered. When I want to complain or whine, I think, *What would Suzanne do?* She can no longer leave the house, jump in the car, and drive somewhere; she constantly relies on others, and some days she's literally stuck. Yet she still exhibits joy and works hard to help others. I'm not physically challenged, and yet I find myself at times easily defeated or irritated or complaining. When this happens, I think of her.

The first people I brag to about God's intervention is my kids. I want them to have front-row seats to God's activity in my life. If God answers a prayer, I tell them. If an unexpected check comes in the mail, and it just happens to match that month's needs, I tell them. When I experience a providential circumstance too big to be a coincidence, I tell them.

Recently I was passing the neighborhood I grew up in when an old friend came to mind. The more I prayed for him, the more I felt compelled to stop by his old house. We hadn't talked to each other in over ten years, so it was odd to have him on my mind. Unable to shake this urge, I made a detour. I knocked on the front door, and his dad answered. When I asked about his son, he offered to call him at work.

My friend got on the phone and said, "You are never going to believe this! I was just trying to track you down online, but I wasn't having any luck. I can't believe you called me! How ironic that after ten years I decide to look you up on social media, and you call me at that exact moment."

This friend didn't know what he believed about God, but this experience gave him hope that maybe God is not only real but cares about him. You better believe I rushed home to share this story with my kids. I want them to know that God is not just the God of Abraham, Isaac, and Jacob. He's the God of Dan, Caleb, Connor, and Colton. He's not just the past-tense God of the Bible or the God you will meet one day after you die. He is also the present-tense God. It's easier for me to convince them of this when they not only hear about God's activity in the Bible but they see God's activity in my life. My life and salvation become symbols of hope for them.

> *Your life may never be made into a Hollywood movie, but it can inspire hope in others.*

Your life may never be made into a Hollywood movie, but

it can inspire hope in others. In the words of the apocalyptic writer John, "They triumphed over him by the blood of the Lamb and by the word of their testimony; they did not love their lives so much as to shrink from death" (Rev. 12:11).

Christians who have walked through decades of marriage can give hope that "till death do us part" is possible.

A follower of Christ living in sobriety can give hope that freedom from addiction is achievable.

A person's redemption story can give hope that God can "save a wretch like me."

A woman or man faithfully serving Christ can give hope that finishing strong is possible.

One of the ladies in our church works for a women's shelter. We routinely donate pajamas and other needed items. A single mom and her two daughters checked into the shelter, and the mom was embarrassed because she didn't have any pajamas for the girls. Our friend was able to grab a brand-new pair for each of them. They matched and were both the right size. The girls began to dance around, because they had never owned a pair of their own pj's. In a culture where kids get upset if they don't get the latest and greatest for Christmas, these two girls were over the moon about something others take for granted. My friend got to be their hero that night. She is a reminder that there is still hope in the world.

How are you living as a symbol of hope?

Chapter 19

MOVING AT THE SPEED OF LIGHT

Recently, I've been thinking about the Flash—not to be confused with Flash Gordon. I'm talking about Barry Allen. Comic book fans will argue that he's the fastest superhero in the comic book universe. While Superman can travel faster than a speeding bullet, the Flash can travel faster than the speed of light, jumping between dimensions and time. He could run around the world and pat himself on the back.

He's the one hero I think our culture is most like. We keep trying to move faster and faster. We want faster downloads, faster travel time, and faster food. Not quality food, just fast food. Every year the pace of life seems to accelerate. This is most likely a direct correlation to all the places we are trying to get to in a day. We find ourselves rushing to fit everything in. When you ask a person how they are doing, the most common answer is busy.

How busy have you been lately? Do you ever drive over the speed limit? Do you ever get annoyed with the internet moving too slowly? Do you hate waiting in lines? Do you wish these chapters were shorter? Personally, I tend to do everything as fast as possible. I count the number of items in each person's cart in the express lane at the grocery store to make sure no one is cheating. I have been known to lock my wife in the car on several occasions because I hit the lock button before she had the chance to even open her car door.

We take our first steps between the ages of nine months and eighteen months, and walking quickly becomes running. Toddlers don't stroll toward a cookie, they run. If you set them down in the store, you just hope you had enough caffeine that morning to keep up with them. Cross training shoes, don't fail me now!

We were made to move, and at times, move fast. Busyness doesn't have to equal ungodliness. Jesus tended to use busy people. The first four guys He recruited were professional fishermen, and Jesus interrupted their work day. He didn't wait until their day off before challenging them to leave their trade to do ministry.

We never see Jesus call a person who's in the midst of a nap. Not that He's against naps (the Lord knows I love them), but He's not first and foremost the "siesta Savior." The pattern in creation is not creation on one day and recreation during the next six. God never tells His people the goal of life is to reach retirement so you can finally truly live. The first book on church history is called the book of Acts, not the book of meetings.

When Jesus asked His disciples to follow Him, they had to lace up their shoes and get ready to keep up. One historian said that Jesus averaged twenty miles a day.[1] Ministry was a marathon. We don't know Jesus' shoe size, but we know He left an impressive footprint everywhere He went. Over the next three years, Jesus would be covered in dust and destiny. Our Savior never stayed in one spot very long. Jesus had a different kind of ADD: A Divine Destiny. When you have a divine destiny, you cannot sit still.

The disciples were constantly on the heels of the One who heals. They left wonder and worship in their wake everywhere they went. People praised God as Jesus kicked demons out of town, healed lepers so they could hug loved ones once again, and turned funerals into parties by bringing the dead back to life. A "sinful woman" kissed Jesus' feet and poured top-shelf perfume on them, and He set her free from a life of slavery to sin.

Jesus would never run from a problem. He marched intentionally into the desert to go toe-to-toe with the one who led mankind astray. Jesus snatched souls from death's grip, walked on water, and trudged up the hill to Calvary, to rest lifeless on a splintered cross before walking triumphantly out of an empty grave. Following in the footsteps of Jesus could lead to a life of miracles and martyrdom. But as Isaiah poetically proclaimed, "How beautiful on the mountains are the feet of those who bring good news, who proclaim peace, who bring good tidings, who proclaim salvation" (Isa. 52:7). In the Old Testament, the phrase used to describe a close relationship with God was one of movement: "Enoch walked faithfully with God" (Gen. 5:24) and "Noah . . . walked faithfully with God" (Gen. 6:9).

As King, God has every right to just sit on a throne. He could be the ultimate couch coach. God could sit in a corner office bossing everyone else around. But ever since He breathed life into mankind's lungs, He has insisted on walking and working with us. He went so far as to choose the route of incarnation rather than delegation—God walking with man.

The verse, "Be still, and know that I am God" (Ps. 46:10) is not about power napping. The word *still* is not directed at our feet but at our heart. It's how Jesus could be insanely busy at times but never insane. His heart was at rest. While His hands were healing, reaching out, He made sure His spirit was full before His schedule was full. "Very early in the morning, while it was still dark, Jesus got up, left the house and went off to a solitary place, where he prayed" (Mark 1:35).

Though we are not given a play-by-play of Jesus' schedule, the gospel writers Matthew, Mark, Luke, and John give us the equivalent of a blockbuster movie trailer. We see the action-packed highlights of Jesus' life and ministry. The Gospels may not tell us all the things we want to know about Jesus, but they include all the things we need to know. One of Mark's favorite ways to describe the pace of Jesus' story is with the words *immediately* or *at once*, which appear forty-one times throughout his gospel.[2] Just after the power of the Holy Spirit descends upon Jesus during His baptism in Mark 1, we learn that "*at once* the Spirit sent him out into the wilderness, and he was in the wilderness forty days, being tested by Satan" (Mark 1:12–13). When you read all sixteen chapters in one sitting, the pace can be breathtaking.

We don't know how busy the average day was for Jesus, but we do know that He faced busy days and seasons. Some of His days were as strained as the waistband on the Incredible Hulk's purple pants. Here are just a few examples. Just about every time Jesus tried to escape the crowds, people acted like they were playing an involuntary game of hide-and-seek (see Matt. 12:15 and 15:21–22). After Jesus found out that John the Baptist had been beheaded, "he withdrew by boat privately to a solitary place. Hearing of this, the crowds followed him on foot from the towns" (Matt. 14:13). John the Baptist had been ruthlessly executed, so Jesus tried to escape to mourn privately. John wasn't just the hype man, setting the stage for Jesus' ministry, he was a friend—and cousin—whom Jesus loved and respected. Despite His efforts, people tracked Him down and disturbed His rest. Instead of blowing up or blowing them off, Jesus seamlessly shifted from grieving to healing mode. Jesus seemed to have an all-you-can-eat buffet of patience. This was just one more way He practiced servanthood, and this moment of surrender led to one of His greatest miracles: He fed the five thousand with five loaves of bread and two fish (see Matt. 14:15–20).

While many of us prioritize ourselves over others and God, Jesus lived an inverted life. He truly put God first, others second, and Himself last. When you live that way, people often think you're a few nuggets short of a Happy Meal. On several occasions, Jesus was so focused on feeding people spiritual food that He neglected to feed Himself (see Mark 6:31 and John 4:31–34). Shortly after appointing the twelve disciples, we read that "Jesus entered a house, and again a crowd gathered, so that he and his disciples were not even able to eat. When his family heard about this, they went to take charge of him, for they said, 'He is out of his mind'" (Mark 3:20–21). His family didn't toss Him a snack just in case He was a little "hangry." No, they literally thought He'd lost His mind because He was preoccupied with ministering to the crowds.

Even after a late night of healing people, Jesus often woke up before everyone else to sneak off for some time with God. Now I'm not naturally a morning person. Before I had kids, I didn't know that five o'clock came twice a day. But Jesus was willing to sacrifice sleep because He knew how important it was to spend time alone in prayer: "Very early in the morning, while it was still dark, Jesus got up, left the house and went off to a solitary place, where he prayed" (Mark 1:35).

When we follow Jesus, we may occasionally have to skip a meal, stay up past our bedtime, heal on Sunday, embrace an interruption, tolerate a critic, or travel far from home. But I find that more often after becoming a Christian, "sit" happens. We sit through church services, small groups, discipleship classes, conferences, and concerts. The early church was too legit to sit. Now granted, I'm being slightly hyperbolic. Of course, the early church also had occasion to sit together: "Every day they continued to meet together in the temple courts. They broke bread in their homes and ate together with glad and sincere hearts" (Acts 2:46). And meetings can be important settings for us to celebrate God's presence, truth, motivation, and strength. But the early church balanced reflection with action. They gathered together for reflection and fellowship, but then went out to respond like missionaries. We become out of balance when too much emphasis is placed on going to church rather than on being the church.

> *We become out of balance when too much emphasis is placed on going to church rather than on being the church.*

Christianity was never meant to become *chair*-ianity. The early church only sat long enough for motivation and education, then they went out and inspired transformation. In Acts chapter 1, we see them gathered together to pray. In Acts chapter 2, they are outside the upper room preaching. In Acts 6:1–7, we see the church huddled together to trouble-shoot a challenge they are having with volunteers and meeting needs. In Acts 6:8 through Acts 7:53, Stephen is outside giving a searing speech to the stiff-necked and religiously comfortable. In Acts 13:1–3, we see a church service where Saul (the apostle Paul) is singled out by the Holy Spirit. In Acts 13:4 through Acts 14:28, Saul goes on his first missionary journey.

We see this pattern of meetings and mission, meetings and mission. The church was too busy locking arms with God and changing the world to sit for any length of time. Even while Paul was imprisoned, he didn't treat that time as a staycation, but rather shared Jesus with other prisoners and wrote four of the New Testament letters.

There are two words that drove the first thirty years of church history: *go* and *wait*. Jesus instructed, "*Go* and make disciples" (Matt. 28:19) and "*Wait* for the gift my Father promised" (Acts 1:4). You can't have the Great Commission without the great *submission*. While the first admonition to go is easy for me, waiting is hard. I enjoy living life at the speed of the Flash. I'd prefer to keep my running shoes on always. But even the Flash must refuel. We need a healthy balance of work and rest, mission and margin, doing and being. The rhythm of life should be one of run and rest. At our breakneck speed, we are often running on empty. We are outrunning our souls. Every hero needs to recharge.

Superman needs earth's yellow sun to stay fueled.

The Flash needs calories.

The Hulk needs anger; the madder he gets, the stronger he is.

The Green Lantern needs to routinely recharge his power ring with the green lantern.

As Christians, we need to routinely spend time with God in order to recharge spiritually. We should never get so focused on working for God that we forget to work *with* God. While we were made to move, we should move at the speed of *His* light.

One of the things I love most about my smartphone is the flashlight feature. I was at the church late one night, and our family pastor saw me on the security camera and decided to prank me. He shut off all the lights in the building. My church feels more like a haunted house than sacred space at night. I consider myself pretty brave, but I might scream at the top of my lungs if I'm there all alone and someone starts moving behind me. Thankfully, I was able to pull out my phone and instantly shine a light. But what would have happened if I hadn't charged my phone? The app wouldn't have worked. Jesus says we are "the light of the world" (Matt. 5:14). But like our phones, we need to plug into the power source in order to light the world effectively.

The number two deathbed regret is "I wish I didn't work so much."[3] Very few people look back on their lives and wish they had put in more overtime. God wants us to have margin in our schedule. In the creation account, God worked for six days and then rested on the seventh. After each day of creation, there was a pause for contemplation and celebration as God announced that His creative work was good (see Gen. 1).

In the same way, we were created to work hard but then to pause for reflection, rejoicing, relationships, and rest. Some of us are better at taking care of others then at taking care of ourselves. Scripture says things like, "In vain you rise early and stay up late, toiling for food to eat—for he grants sleep to those he loves" (Ps. 127:2). He grants sleep to those He loves. The older I get, the more I appreciate a good power nap. On the other hand, my wife hates napping. According to Psalm 127, God loves me more than her. All joking aside, God wired us with a need to rest.

Pastor, speaker, and author Craig Groeschel said, "Most of us are living at a pace that is not only unsustainable; it's also unbiblical."[4] Most people are too distracted by the wrong things to notice the blessings God has for them. When is the last time you embraced a beautiful moment, read to your kids, went on a date night, looked up at the stars, or laughed until you snorted out milk?

Heroes need to practice going and waiting. Sometimes we need a push to get off our seats while other times we need a reminder to rest.

Now I'm a busy guy. I'm married with three kids. Because my wife is legally blind, I do all the driving. I'm the lead pastor of a church I started, and I serve on a few boards. I mentor young pastors on a monthly basis. I'm also a writer, which means blogging, tweeting, posting to Instagram, and editing, editing, editing. Some days I feel like an unpaid Uber driver as I make trips to school, karate, friends' houses, etc. When you have a toddler, trips are never as simple as driving from point A to point B. When we are near a toilet, my youngest doesn't have to go. As soon as we are thirty minutes from the nearest bathroom, suddenly it's operation pee-pee dance. The excursion becomes a tour de toilet as we hunt for the nearest facility, which is inevitably a restroom where I don't want him to touch anything, and I wish I could set off a hand-sanitizer bomb. But while my schedule reaches a fever pitch at times, I have discovered two principles and two practices that help me balance work and rest.

Principle One: Where God guides, He provides. I truly believe that if I'm following God's lead, He will give me the energy, time, and resources needed to accomplish each God-inspired goal. In the words of Paul, "I can do all this through him who gives me strength" (Phil. 4:13).

> *Where God guides, He provides.*

Practice One: Start the day with God. I'm at my best when I'm not at the mercy of the calendar or clock. I do this by starting the day in prayer and quiet reflection on truths like, "The LORD is my shepherd, I lack nothing" (Ps. 23:1). I have a spot down by the lake where I love to start my day with repentance, rejoicing, and rest. For me, resting leads to trusting. I'm reminded that God doesn't need me to solve all of the world's problems.

When I look out across Lake Michigan, I'm reminded that God created a lake so big I can't see across it and that He did that without me. And that's only a piece of all that God has created. God set the world in motion without my input, He has rescued billions of lives without my prayers or preaching, and God won't retire when I expire. The kingdom will still advance, souls will be saved, lives will be changed, and I will most likely be forgotten in a few generations. In spite of my cosmic insignificance, God created me, called me, and gives

> *I can handle my schedule when I manage my soul.*

purpose to my life. My days are more manageable when I remind myself of these truths.

Principle Two: I can handle my schedule when I manage my soul. When I'm getting the sleep, exercise, nutrients, recreation, and time with God I need, I can work hard, accomplish goals, and not become overwhelmed. I think of this as charging my internal batteries. When I've let any of these things slide, my battery gets low and my days feel like an endless game of Monopoly where I just keep passing Go and wish I would be sent to jail for a mini break. When I'm stressed, I look at the state of my soul before I look at the pace of my schedule.

Practice Two: Compartmentalize. I've been asked several times how I managed to write a book with such a packed schedule. The answer is that I compartmentalize my day. For three months, I committed to write each night from eight o'clock until midnight. I gave up TV and the internet during that time period. I now treat my whole day that way.

In order to spend quality time with my family, I leave my work at the office (which is not easy to do when you're a pastor and everyone in your church has your number). When I'm on a date with my wife, I keep my phone in my pocket on vibrate. It helps that I wear skinny jeans . . . and since pockets on skinny jeans are more decorative than functional, I can't pull my phone out fast enough to take a call. When I guard my schedule in this way, it's a lot easier to know when it's time to focus on work and when it's time to rest, reflect, and relate.

Have you been serving at the speed of light?

Chapter 20

YOUR
GREATEST
VILLAIN

D o you feel beach-ready or, like me, are you just planning to wear a T-shirt in the pool this year? Maybe your six-pack is still hibernating under a cave of carbs. Maybe there's a little jiggle when you wiggle. I've heard that only 1 in 20,000 people have a visible six-pack. Most of us will never be able to post the coveted six-pack selfie on social media, unless we airbrush it. Yet every comic book hero has chiseled abs. Heroes in the Marvel and DC universe don't typically have dad and mom bods; they don't have stretch marks and cellulite. They don't have to wear stretchy pants at Thanksgiving. They look like Greek gods.

As summer approaches, people start thinking they want

that same hero look. They buy gym memberships and start a new diet. Or they buy some expensive running shoes that they wear once or twice before dumping them in a closet where they wait to be donated to charity. While gyms are part of an industry that earns $21 billion a year, 80 percent of the people with gym memberships never go.[1] The only thing getting thinner each month is their wallet.

Fortunately for us, we don't have to look good in tights to be a superhero. The muscle that matters most is our heart and how big it is. The word *heart* in Scripture refers to the core of who we are—our thoughts, feelings, and will. It's the reason why we are challenged to love God with all of our heart. When we allow our inner life to drift, it begins to take a toll on our outer life. A hero must fight to keep his or her heart right to successfully fight for families and friends. We must protect our character if we are going to be effective at protecting the city.

> *We must protect our character if we are going to be effective at protecting the city.*

There's a reason why Paul emphasizes character over competence (see 1 Tim. 3) when looking for leaders to make a difference in the world. There has been a long line of people with sky-high skills who have ruined their lives and the lives of others because of a bankrupt inner life. Sometimes we are our own worst enemy.

Recently, I was at the gym when a guy came in wearing his work clothes: jeans, button-up shirt, and steel-toed boots. People choose to wear a lot of interesting outfits while working out, but this guy's clothes were neither fashionable nor functional. Squats are hard enough when you're not wearing jeans. He loaded up a couple of forty-five-pound plates onto a barbell and bent over to do some deadlifts with his back rounded like a crescent moon (not the ideal spine shape while lifting heavy objects). His muscles were taut, determination showed on his face, and he strained like someone "unworthy" trying to lift Thor's hammer . . . but the bar didn't budge. Sheepishly, he looked around to see if anyone had noticed. Fortunately, he didn't see the look on my face. Rather than remove some weight, he tried again. Nothing. He tried a third time, and the bar miraculously inched up to the level of his shins. He dropped it to the ground, proudly announcing, "I did it!" The only thing he did was ensure a future of back problems and pain. He was his own worst enemy.

There are moments when it would be great to have super-human strength—when you're trying to deadlift too much and people are secretly watching you. Or when you need to stop a bully, lift a car off someone trapped underneath, or just carry the groceries inside in a single trip. While there are a lot of comic book heroes with legendary strength, there is only one person in the Bible who had that gift. His name was Samson. There's a phrase that is repeated throughout his story: "the Spirit of the LORD came powerfully upon him" (Judg. 14:6, 19; 15:14). He did not get this power in the gym, he got it from God.

There are several examples of Samson's physical strength. He went toe-to-toe with a lion and didn't become a Manwich. If you're out in the wild and get attacked by a wild animal, you hope it's a koala, emu, or sloth, but not a lion. There's a reason why lions are called the "king of the jungle." They are at the top of the food chain. They don't struggle with anxiety and fear. If it had been a fair fight, Samson would certainly have become kitty kibble. But Samson plus the Spirit of the Lord equals victory every time. The king of the jungle meets the King of kings. And the predator became the prey. Samson won hands down.

At one point, Samson was trapped because he had disobeyed God. Huge doors blocked him from escaping the city. But when your biceps look nine months pregnant, you don't need a key. He ripped the doors off of the city gate, which probably weighed hundreds of pounds, and carried the gate to the top of a hill. He could have just set it to the side but instead the gates became a billboard advertising his strength and sending the message "Unstoppable."

Now if you were foolish enough to fight Samson, you might want to bring a few of your friends, ideally your big, not-afraid-to-fight-dirty friends. One of the most impressive displays of Samson's strength was when he was attacked by a crowd of soldiers. I imagine it being like a scene from one of those cheesy martial arts movies. Samson was surrounded by a thousand men, and it looked like he might be about to experience his first loss. Instead, he grabbed the jawbone of a donkey and created a story none of those guys would want to go home and tell their wives (see Judg. 15).

"Honey, how did you get that black eye?"

"I don't want to talk about it."

Samson truly was unstoppable, at least physically. But every superhero has a weakness.

For the Man of Steel, it's kryptonite.

For the Green Lantern, it's the color yellow.

For Wolverine, it's magnets.

For Samson, it's a lustful heart.

In the 1940s, Wonder Woman came on the comic book scene, and she was the only female at the time to have her own feature-length comic book. Her main weapons are a lasso of truth and some bulletproof bracelets, and she is as strong as Superman. But like most heroes, Wonder Woman has a weakness. Normally she can win an arm wrestling contest against the entire Justice League, but if her bracelets are chained together by a man, she is rendered powerless.

> *God loves using weaklings to do the impossible.*

Many of us struggle with some monumental weaknesses, but God loves using weaklings to do the impossible. Samson had his weakness, as well. He was given his strength to protect God's people and was instructed to avoid two things in the book of Judges, and possibly a third based on the Nazarite vow in Numbers 6. In order to maintain his strength, he had to avoid: alcoholic beverages, barber shops, and possibly dead bodies (though this is not expressly communicated in Judges). But he would end up violating all three of those requirements. He went to a party and got hammered, and he not only got close to a dead lion carcass but he ate some honey from inside of it (ew!). So, the climactic haircut is just the final compromise.

As long as Samson's hair was long, he was strong like King Kong. But because of his love/lust for Delilah, he told her the secret to his strength after she kept nagging him for the truth. It didn't help that Delilah intentionally set a trap for him. She cut his hair while he was sleeping, and he was then attacked by a handful of soldiers. Some of the saddest words in the Bible are: "He awoke from his sleep and thought, 'I'll go out as before and shake myself free.' But he did not know that the LORD had left him" (Judg. 16:20). He did not know that the Lord had left him. He had unplugged from God and lost his power.

One thing to ask based on the story of Samson is this: What are you allowing into your life that threatens to prevent God's power from working through you? Think about the pastors, politicians, professors, and performers who have lost their voice because they pursued the wrong things. They followed their shadow side. I'm often shocked at how much darkness still lurks in my heart.

For example, not too long ago, my dog got into the garbage. It has a lid on it, but she figured out how to nose it open. When I went to take the scraps away from her, she barked aggressively and then snipped at me. She had never bitten me before. Instinctively, I said a naughty word. I was shocked. I didn't know that vocabulary was still in there. But as surprised as I was, the dog was even more startled. Instantly, Chloe knew she blew it. If Pastor Dan is swearing, the lightning of God must be next. She put herself in time out. I would have laughed if I wasn't so angry. First I was angry at her for biting me, and second, I was mad at myself for allowing my temper to dig up something dark from within.

While Samson decisively beat the three-hundred-pound lion that threatened his life, there was another lion that went after his God-given potential. This lion has feasted on the hopes and dreams of men and women since the garden. We never see this beast overtly in the story of Samson. But like any skilled predator, he's there hiding in the shadows; he's behind every temptation, ready to pounce. This "lion" successfully attacked Samson through the temptation of lust.

As it says in 1 Peter 5:8, "Your enemy the devil prowls around like a roaring lion looking for someone to devour." We see him devouring lives through pornography, sex trafficking, gang activity, and police brutality but also in snapping at the barista, hating on the person who got the shoes you couldn't afford, and flirting with a coworker. When Samson compromised his character, he lost his competence. More heroes have been brought down by weak values than villains.

When I was a kid, I had a friend who was obsessed with the Civil War. And I'm not talking about Marvel's *Civil War*. He memorized the Gettysburg Address and insisted on reciting it every time we played kids' war games. One day, he had the terrible idea of reenacting a hanging. There was a rope attached to a tree in my yard. So he propped a skateboard against the tree, stood on it, and tied the rope around his neck. What could go wrong? Then the skateboard slipped, and he began to dangle. His eyes bulged; his feet kicked. Fortunately, I ran over and was able to lift him up on my shoulders and untie the rope. Gasping and crying, he ran home. "Does that mean you forfeit the battle?" I called.

After he left, I was trying to figure out how the skateboard slipped from under him. So, I climbed up on it and put the rope around my own neck . . . not one of my brightest moments. Sure enough, I started to dangle. But my friend wasn't around to save me. Thankfully, the rope wasn't tied tightly enough so it came loose, and I ended up with a nasty rope burn around my neck. That was the last time I played war games as a kid.

I tell this embarrassing story because sometimes we are a lot better at helping others than we are at helping ourselves. We help others find freedom from addiction but secretly we struggle. We tell our friends to dump that toxic guy or girl, but we can't let go of our own poisonous partner. We lead a Bible study teaching others about serving God, but it's been a while since we've cracked a Bible open ourselves, prayed, or fasted.

Before you can save the city, you need Christ to save you . . . especially from yourself.

Chapter 21

THE POWER OF LEGACY

Have you ever felt unqualified?

While I was writing this book, my personal hero died. My grandpa was one of only three people I knew who could rock a mustache: Tom Selleck, Yosemite Sam, and Grandpa. Even when cancer robbed him of his head of hair, he still had his formidable 'stache. Not only did he have impressive facial hair, he also modeled morality and manliness. He once said, "My goal is not only to go to heaven someday but to bring a little heaven down every day." My grandpa did that for me.

Growing up, I always thought his house was a mansion. When your own house is so small you step from the front door into the backyard, every other house feels like a mansion.

There was enough room at Grandpa's house for everyone to come over for the holidays. Adults got to sit at the big table, and all the cousins gathered around the kids' table. Every holiday I was promised next year I'd get to sit at the adult table. I'm now forty, and I still sit at the kids' table.

There was one room in which Grandpa spent most of his time: his office. He would spend hours in that room surrounded by books. It was his sanctuary and the place where he worked, studied, and lectured his kids and eventually his grandkids. His preferred form of punishment was an hour-long monologue. Between the mustache and monologue, he would have made a great villain. But the thing he did most often in that room was pray. His first reaction to all of life's challenges was to get on his knees. He knew that an hour in his "prayer closet" would do a whole lot more than an hour on a soapbox.

When I was eighteen and morally lost, I prayed the agnostic prayer, "God, I don't know if You're real, but if You are, I need You to come to my rescue." That very week, Grandpa came down from his cabin in Crivitz, Wisconsin. If you have ever been lost, you know what it is like to live in Crivitz, because it is in the middle of nowhere. Ironically, God would use that middle-of-nowhere location to give my life direction.

Without knowing about my desperate prayer, my grandpa said to me, "While I was praying, I felt like God told me I was supposed to ask you to come live with me." As someone once said, "Coincidence is God's way of staying anonymous." For the first time in my life, I felt like God was real and had heard my prayer. It was at my grandpa's home that my life changed. If it were not for my grandpa, I probably would not be around—physically or spiritually.

His legacy was different than my dad's.

When my dad died, he left me his pickup truck. My dad was a cowboy at heart, and he loved John Wayne and Clint Eastwood. He rode horses, loved country music, and wore cowboy boots, Wrangler jeans, and a Stetson hat. His truck smelled like him, a combination of Old Spice and Marlboro cigarettes. Anytime I drove that truck, it was like he was riding shotgun.

When my grandpa died, he left me one of his Bibles. He had underlined all the verses he loved. He would have saved on ink if he would have just underlined the ones he didn't like. He was constantly in the Word and the Word was in him. Grandpa was like the Scripture version of Siri. You could ask him any question about the Bible, and if you had four hours to spare, he had four hours' worth of answers.

The Bible was handed to me at his funeral. The weight of that Bible represented to me the weight of his role in our family. He was the patriarch. He was the one everyone went to when they had a question or needed prayer or a place to stay. There are people whose relation to me I still question because Grandpa constantly took people in. Standing near the casket and receiving one of his Bibles, I felt like a little kid standing in his dad's shoes.

Later in my grandpa's life, he had an odd experience. One evening, he spontaneously woke up in the middle of the night. He felt like God was nudging him to get up and pray. But like most people, he enjoyed sleep and was tempted to just roll back over. So he said, "If I look over at the clock and it says 3:33 a.m., I'll get up." He looked over at the clock and to his surprise it was 3:33 a.m. I picture God laughing at my grandpa's holy dare. That same experience happened a half dozen times throughout his last several years.

A few weeks after his funeral I had to travel to a conference. Late that night, I spontaneously woke up and looked at the clock. To my shock, the time read 3:33 a.m. In that moment, I sensed God saying to me, "I need you to carry on the work I did in and through your grandpa." I felt like I was inheriting a legacy and felt woefully unqualified. Elisha must have felt the same when the prophet Elijah put his prophetic cloak around him, symbolizing his need to carry on the prophet's message, mission, and miracles. First, I was handed my grandpa's Bible, and second, I was given my grandpa's prayer pattern.

Every generation passes things along to the next generation. Think about the legacy of Superman. He has been around since 1938 and looks amazing for a senior citizen. The red cape has been donned by the barrel-chested George Reeves, the slender Christopher Reeve, and the "I can't keep my shirt on" Henry Cavill, among others. The red and blue tights have been passed on from generation to generation. Senior citizens and seniors in high school alike can finish his catchphrase, "It's a bird, it's a plane, it's Superman!"

Legacy is one of the ways in which we outlive ourselves. Sometimes we pass along a financial debt, a receding hairline, a favorite sports team, or a history-making document like the Emancipation Proclamation. But the most important thing we can pass along to the next generation is a robust relationship with God.

We see this passing on of the faith through spiritual relationships such as:

Moses and Joshua
Mordecai and Esther
Naomi and Ruth
Barnabas and Paul
Paul and Timothy
Batman and Robin
(Just seeing if you're still paying attention.)

> *The most important thing we can pass along to the next generation is a robust relationship with God.*

While many people might wish they could inherit a million dollars from a rich aunt or uncle and some would even settle for a hundred dollars, the questions I wrestle with are, "What will the next generation inherit when I die? What will I leave my kids?"

The answer lies in the words of David: "Since my youth, God, you have taught me, and to this day I declare your marvelous deeds. Even when I am old and gray, do not forsake me, my God, till I declare your power to the next generation, your mighty acts to all who are to come" (Ps. 71:17–18).

Like the generations before me, I want to heroically pass the power of God on to the next generation.

A college friend of mine recently had a double lung and

heart transplant. He's one of those guys who is a relentless optimist. You can't help but feel elevated when you spend time with him. He has the kind of generous heart you wish could be transplanted into every living being. There were several times when he was in the hospital essentially dying and yet still took the time to get others a cup of coffee. There's a picture on his Facebook page of him holding up a sign that says: One organ donor can save eight lives, and I'm one of them.

Because one person put a checkmark on their driver's license, he gets a second chance at life. He gets to watch his little girls grow up. When the anonymous person agreed to be an organ donor when they died, they had no idea what kind of life and legacy that would create. They never met my friend; they didn't know what kind of impact their decision would make. In the same way, we have no idea how monumental our small acts of kindness and sacrifices might be or the lives that might be touched by them.

Changing the world doesn't start with a cape and a catchphrase. Changing the world starts by allowing God to invade your world. Those in the early church discovered that you don't need an S on your chest if you have the Savior in your heart. And if they had a catchphrase, it was the five words, "They had been with Jesus."[1] That was all they needed to go from ordinary to extraordinary. They were inspired by Christ's resurrection to not just go to church on Sundays but to be the church all week long. They turned their world upside down through sharing and showing Jesus. In just thirty years, between Acts chapters 1 and 28, the church swelled in numbers. What could we accomplish in our lifetime if we took the gospel that seriously?

Whenever my kids watch the latest Marvel or DC movie, they walk away inspired. They talk about the movie, they go home and role-play, and they debate which hero is the most powerful. In the same way, Easter is supposed to inspire us and shape the way we live. It's interesting that the disciples didn't make it a practice to go back to the tomb yearly but instead honored the death of Jesus by living out the Great Commission *daily*. Listen to Paul's impassioned words, "I want to know Christ and the power that raised him from the dead. I want to share in his sufferings and become like him in his death" (Phil. 3:10 NCV). When Easter goes from a holiday to a holy day, it's a day that reminds us that through the cross and resurrection, suffering and triumph, we have grace for our failures and hope for our future.

A question we need to wrestle with is this: are we experiencing the power of Christ's resurrection? Is Easter having a tangible impact on our everyday life? Would our life look any different if Easter never happened? I can live without Thanksgiving, Valentine's Day, and Groundhog Day, but can I live without Easter? The early church didn't celebrate once a year, they celebrated every time they gathered, took communion, or baptized; like Paul, they also "want[ed] to know Christ" and "the power of his resurrection" (Phil. 3:10). Does my life revolve around the resurrection's power as well?

God wants to do something powerful in you and through you, but you must be open to His lordship. The resurrection shows us that "it is finished" doesn't mean it is final. God can turn the impossible into the inevitable. Nope into hope.

When we allow our lives to be shaped by the resurrection, we become incurable optimists. We believe to the core of our being that God can change our world. We stop just reading about miracles, and we start experiencing them. We become an answer to other people's prayers. We create a legacy our family and friends desperately need to inherit.

Just like Moses handed his legacy over to Joshua.

Elijah handed his over to Elisha.

Mordecai handed his over to Esther.

Jesus handed His over to the disciples.

My grandpa handed his over to me.

> The resurrection shows us that "it is finished" doesn't mean it is final. God can turn the impossible into the inevitable.

A legacy is being placed into your hands; now you must decide what you are going to do with it. When the prophet Elijah was ready to "retire," he dropped his cloak, the same prophetic hoodie he had just used to part the Red Sea. His protégé Elisha picked it up as a symbol of carrying on his legacy (see 2 Kings 2).

Just because the missionary dies doesn't mean the mission dies. Just because the messenger of God dies doesn't mean the message is silenced. When the prophet dropped the mic, the next generation had the opportunity to pick it up. While Elijah performed fourteen miracles, Elisha would go on to perform twenty-eight. Elisha asked for a double portion and had double the impact.

Currently a generation of godly men and women are making their exit. Symbolically they are leaving behind their cloaks. Will we courageously carry on their legacy? Will we drop the cape and pick up the cloak? The cape represents superpowers, but the cloak represents spiritual empowerment.

> *Lose the cape, accept the mission God has given you, and show the world what happens when the ordinary rise.*

The world doesn't need another superhero; the world needs you and me to carry on the legacy handed down to us by ordinary men and women who accomplished extraordinary things. Are you ready to be the hands and feet of Jesus? Are you ready to pass the power of God to the next generation?

We started this book with the question, "Who am I?"

You are a hero.

Your superpower is Jesus.

Your catchphrase is "Thy will be done."

Your mission is to make the world a better place through presence, prayer, and perseverance.

Lose the cape, accept the mission God has given you, and show the world what happens when the ordinary rise.

NOTES

Chapter 1: Your Not-So-Secret Identity

1. "Identity Theft Victim Statistics," *Identity Theft and Scam Prevention Services*, 2007–2017, http://www.identitytheft.info/victims.aspx.
2. Juan Martin Ponce, "The History of Superman's Power," Man of Steel Answers Insight Commentary (blog), November 13, 2014, http://www.manofsteelanswers.com/the-history-of-supermans-powers-fanzig/.
3. "Hulk (comics)," *Wikipedia*, last modified November 9, 2017, https://en.wikipedia.org/wiki/Hulk_(comics).
4. Chris Sims, "Guns and the Batman: Why the Dark Knight Doesn't Use Firearms," *Comics Alliance*, January 17, 2013, http://comicsalliance.com/batman-guns-gun-culture/.

Chapter 2: When the Ordinary Rise

1. D. L. Cade, "Disney Used to Photoshop Out Cigarettes in Portraits of Walt Disney," *Peta Pixel*, October 12, 2016, https://petapixel.com/2016/10/12/disneyland-used-photoshop-cigarettes-portraits-walt-disney/?ref=webdesignernews.com.
2. "Top 10 Highest Paid Hollywood Actors," *Top 101 News*, http://top101news.com/2015-2016-2017-2018/news/entertainment/celebrities/richest-highest-paid-hollywood-actors/.
3. Sarah Gibson, "These Are the 10 Highest Grossing Movies Ever Worldwide," *High Snobiety*, July 26, 2017, http://www.highsnobiety.com/2017/07/26/highest-grossing-movies/.
4. Beatrice Verhoeven, "17 Highest-Grossing Movies Directed by Women, from 'Mama Mia!' to 'Wonder Woman,'" *The Wrap*, June 22, 2017, http://www.thewrap.com/17-highest-grossing-movies-directed-by-women/.
5. Christie D'Zurilla, "By the numbers, San Diego Comic Con International 2016," *LA Times*, July 24, 2016, http://www.latimes.com/entertainment/la-et-hc-comic-con-updates-by-the-numbers-san-diego-comic-con-1469118665-htmlstory.html.
6. Bradford W. Wright, *Comic Book Nation: The Transformation of Youth Culture in America* (Baltimore: The Johns Hopkins University Press, 2001).
7. Michael E. Uslan, *The Boy Who Loved Batman* (electronic version) (San Francisco: Chronicle Books, 2011), 15.
8. "Rise of the Superhero: From the Golden Age to the Silver Screen," The Editors of Life, *LIFE*, November 10, 2017, 27.
9. *Global Slavery Index 2016*, https://www.globalslaveryindex.org/.

10. Bill Federer, "A Brief History of Slavery," *WND*, February 14, 2017, http://www.wnd.com/2017/02/a-brief-history-of-slavery/.

11. Nick Vujicic, *Unstoppable: The Incredible Power of Faith in Action* (Colorado Springs: Waterbrook, 2013), 139.

12. Kara Warner, "'Dark Knight Rises' Chant Rooted in Real Language, Hans Zimmer Says," *MTV*, July 25, 2012, http://www.mtv.com/news/2600833/dark-knight-rises-hans-zimmer-chanting/.

13. Justin Worland, "The Viral Ice Bucket Challenge Has Raised $15.6 Million for ALS," *TIME*, August 18, 2104, http://time.com/3136458/viral-als-ice-bucket-challenge-funds-raised-15-million/.

14. "400 students sing to teacher fighting cancer," *CNN*, http://www.cnn.com/videos/tv/2016/09/12/students-teacher-cancer-sing-daily-hit-new-day.cnn.

15. "2399. idiótés," *Bible Hub*, http://biblehub.com/greek/2399.htm.

Chapter 3: Underdogs Overcome

1. "Underdog," *Merriam-Webster*, November 10, 2017, http://www.merriam-webster.com/dictionary/underdog.

2. Cork Gaines, "The Cubs are a huge favorite to win the World Series," *Business Insider*, September 12, 2016, http://www.businessinsider.com/world-series-favorites-cubs-2016-9.

3. *Star Wars: Episode V The Empire Strikes Back*, directed by Irvin Kershner (Banks, Oregon: Lucasfilm, 1980), DVD.

4. "The State of the Church 2016," *Barna*, September 15, 2016, https://www.barna.com/research/state-church-2016/.

5. "What percentage of people are considered geniuses?" *CliffsNotes*, https://www.cliffsnotes.com/cliffsnotes/subjects/literature/what-percentage-of-people-are-considered-geniuses.

6. "George W. Bush: C students, you too can be president," *USA Today*, May 17, 2015, https://www.usatoday.com/story/news/nation-now/2015/05/17/george-w-bush-c-students-president-graduation/27488795/.

7. Samuel Arbesman, "The Fraction of Famous People in the World," *WIRED*, January 22, 2013, https://www.wired.com/2013/01/the-fraction-of-famous-people-in-the-world/.

8. "List of biblical names," *Wikipedia*, last modified October 12, 2017, https://en.wikipedia.org/wiki/List_of_biblical_names.

9. Bruce Shelly, *Church History in Plain Language*, Updated 2nd Edition (Nashville: Thomas Nelson, 1995), 163.

Chapter 4: Not Just Heroes and Zeroes

1. Yury Spektorov, Olya Linde, Bart Cornelissen, and Rostislav Khomenko, "The Global Diamond Report 2013: Journey through the Value Chain," *Bain & Company*, August 27, 2013, http://www.bain.com/publications/articles/global-diamond-report-2013.aspx.

2. "Engagement ring," *Wikipedia*, last modified November 9, 2017, https://en.wikipedia.org/wiki/Engagement_ring.

3. Claire Nowak and Kelly Bare, "Here's the Real Reason We Propose with Engagement Rings," *Reader's Digest*, http://www.rd.com/advice/relationships/the-history-of-engagement-rings/.

4. Glenn Singer, "What Does Carbon Do for Human Bodies?" *AZCentral.*, http://healthyliving.azcentral.com/carbon-human-bodies-4307.html.

5. John H. Walton, "Genesis," *The NIV Application Commentary*, (Grand Rapids: Zondervan, 2001), 130.

6. Paul Ferguson, "Adam," *Bible Study Tools*, http://www.biblestudytools.com/dictionary/adam/.

7. Ellen R. Braaf, "Diggin' Dirt," *Education Place*, https://www.eduplace.com/science/hmxs/es/modc/cricket/sect6cc.shtml.

8. "What Are Little Boys Made Of?" *Wikipedia*, last modified November 4, 2017, https://en.wikipedia.org/wiki/What_Are_Little_Boys_Made_Of%3F.

9. "Mona Lisa," *Wikipedia*, last modified November 10, 2017, https://en.wikipedia.org/wiki/Mona_Lisa.

10. Matt Weinberger and Madeline Stone, "19 crazy facts about Bill Gates' $123 million mansion," *Business Insider*, December 16, 2015, http://www.businessinsider.com/19-crazy-facts-about-bill-gates-123-million-house-2015-12.

11. "The 7 Most Expensive Diamonds in the World," *SH Zell & Sons*, http://www.shzell.com/most-expensive-diamonds.

Chapter 5: Created for Adventure

1. "7962. shalvah," *Bible Hub*, http://biblehub.com/hebrew/7962.htm.

2. "Ecclesiastical Property Ownership in the Middle Ages," *Unam Sanctam Catholicam*, http://www.unamsanctamcatholicam.com/history/historical-apologetics/79-history/501-church-owned-land-middle-ages.html.

3. "Francis of Assisi," *Wikipedia*, last modified November 13, 2017, https://en.wikipedia.org/wiki/Francis_of_Assisi.

4. "How Safe Is Flying? Detailed Statistics," *Flying Fear*, June 13, 2009, http://www.flyingfear.net/general/how-safe-is-flying-detailed-statistics.html.

5. *Captain America: The First Avenger*, directed by Joe Johnston (Paramount Pictures, Marvel Entertainment, 2011), DVD.

6. "Great A. A. Milne Quotes," My Town Tutors, January 13, 2014, http://mytowntutors.com/2014/01/great-a-a-milne-quotes/.

Chapter 6: The *Her* in Hero

1. *The Dark Knight Rises*, directed by Christopher Nolan (Warner Bros, Legendary Entertainment, DC Entertainment, 2012), DVD.

2. *Iron Man 3*, directed by Shane Black (Paramount Pictures, Marvel Entertainment, 2013), DVD.

3. *The Amazing Spider-Man 2*, directed by Marc Webb (Marvel Enterprises, Avi Arad Productions, Columbia Pictures, 2014), DVD.

4. "Retinitis pigmentosa," *Genetics Home Reference*, https://ghr.nlm.nih
   .gov/condition/retinitis-pigmentosa.
5. Laura Story, "Blessings," from the album *Blessings*, Fair Trade/
   Columbia, 2011.
6. Nick Vujicic, *Life Without Limits: Inspiration for a Ridiculously Good
   Life* (Colorado Springs: Waterbook, 2012), 21.

Chapter 7: Protect Your City

1. Anna Robaton, "Why so many Americans hate their jobs," *Money
   Watch*, March 31, 2017, http://www.cbsnews.com/news/why-so-many-
   americans-hate-their-jobs/.
2. James Montgomery Boice, *Nehemiah* (Grand Rapids: Baker Books,
   1990), 17.
3. Michael Rydelnik and Michael Vanlaningham, gen eds, *The Moody
   Bible Commentary* (Chicago: Moody, 2014), 654.
4. "Stan Lee," *Wikipedia*, last modified May 19, 2017, https://en.wiki
   quote.org/wiki/Stan_Lee.

Chapter 8: The Original Dynamic Duo

1. Thomas A. Edison, spoken statement, (c. 1903) published in *Harper's
   Monthly*, September, 1932, https://en.wikiquote.org/wiki/Thomas_
   Edison.
2. Todd M. Johnson, "Protestantism after 500 Years," The Exchange,
   Christianity Today, April 3, 2017, http://www.christianitytoday.com/
   edstetzer/2017/march/protestantism-after-500-years.html.
3. "Facts About Water: Statistics of the Water Crisis," *The Water Project*,
   updated August 31, 2016, https://thewaterproject.org/water-scarcity/
   water_stats.
4. "Teresa of Ávila Quotes," *Good Reads*, https://www.goodreads.com/
   quotes/80993-christ-has-no-body-now-on-earth-but-yours-no.
5. "Father Absence + Involvement | Statistics," *National Fatherhood
   Initiative*, https://www.fatherhood.org/fatherhood-data-statistics.
6. C. S. Lewis, *The Great Divorce* (1946; repr., New York: HarperOne,
   2001), 75.

Chapter 9: Justice Comes Down to *Just Us*

1. Richard Stearns, *The Hole in Our Gospel* (Nashville: Thomas Nelson,
   2009), 8–11, 26, 46, 50.
2. *World Vision*, https://www.worldvision.org/sponsorship.
3. *SOS Children's Villages USA*, www.sos-usa.org.
4. Marjorie Ainsborough Decker, "There Was an Old Woman," in *The
   Christian Mother Goose Book of Nursery Rhymes* (New York: Grosset &
   Dunlap, 2001), 7.
5. Iona and Peter Opie, eds., *The Oxford Dictionary of Nursery Rhymes*,
   new edition (Oxford: Oxford University Press, 1997), 522.
6. "100 People: A World Portrait," *100 People*, http://www.100people
   .org/statistics_detailed_statistics.php.

7. Quotes (103) from *The Dark Knight Rises*, IMDb, http://m.imdb
.com/title/tt1345836/quotes?qt=qt1744936.

Chapter 10: A Tragic Beginning

1. Glen Weldon, *The Caped Crusader* (New York: Simon & Schuster,
2016), 14.
2. "Charles R. Swindoll Quotes," *Good Reads*, https://www.goodreads
.com/author/quotes/5139.Charles_R_Swindoll.
3. John H. Walton, "Genesis," *The NIV Application Commentary* (Grand
Rapids: Zondervan, 2001), 666.
4. *Cory's Project*, www.corysproject.com.

Chapter 11: What's in Your Utility Belt?

1. Brian Truitt, "Superman debut comic found in wall sells for
$175,000," *USA Today*, June 13, 2013, http://www.usatoday.com/
story/life/2013/06/13/superman-action-comics-issue-found-in-
wall/2419837/.

Chapter 13: Courage Is Contagious

1. *Ant-Man*, directed by Peyton Reed (Marvel Studios, Walt Disney
Studios Motion Pictures, 2015), DVD.
2. Mark Jenkins, "Maxed Out on Everest," *National Geographic*, June
2013, http://ngm.nationalgeographic.com/2013/06/125-everest-
maxed-out/jenkins-text.
3. "Roger Bannister breaks four-minutes [*sic*] mile," *This Day in History*,
http://www.history.com/this-day-in-history/roger-bannister-breaks-
four-minutes-mile.
4. "Chuck Yeager," *Biography*, last updated September 19, 2016, http://
www.biography.com/people/chuck-yeager-9538831.
5. Robert Z. Pearlman, "Details in Death of Yuri Gagarin, 1st Man in
Space, Revealed 45 Years Later," *Space*, June 17, 2013, http://www
.space.com/21594-yuri-gagarin-death-cause-revealed.html.
6. Matt Sloane, Jason Hanna, and Dana Ford, "'Never, ever give up':
Diana Nyad completes historic Cuba-to-Florida swim," *CNN*, September 3, 2013, http://www.cnn.com/2013/09/02/world/americas/
diana-nyad-cuba-florida-swim/index.html.

Chapter 14: Better Than X-ray Vision

1. "Black Death," *History*, 2010, http://www.history.com/topics/
black-death.
2. Don Joseph Goewey, "85 Percent of What We Worry About Never
Happens," The Blog, *Huffpost*, August 25, 2015 (updated December
6, 2017), https://www.huffingtonpost.com/don-joseph-goewey-/85-
of-what-we-worry-about_b_8028368.html.

Chapter 15: The Original Superpower

1. Lindsay Terry, "Story behind the song: 'It is well with my soul,'" October 16, 2014, http://staugustine.com/living/religion/2014-10-16/story-behind-song-it-well-my-soul.
2. "Martin Luther's speech at the trial of Worms, 1521," *My Personal Journey by Henry Luke* (blog), June 15, 2017, https://thelukejourney.wordpress.com/2017/06/15/martin-luthers-speech-at-the-trial-of-worms-1521/.
3. Tom Rath and Donald O. Clifton, *How Full Is Your Bucket?* (New York: Gallup Press, 2004), 45.
4. "Friedrich Nietzsche Quotes," *Good Reads*, www.goodreads.com/quotes/108811-all-i-need-is-a-sheet-of-paper-and-something.

Chapter 16: The Power of Perseverance

1. Alistair Wearmouth, "Our Backyard: Black Hills National Forest," *Backpacker*, December 10, 2010, http://www.backpacker.com/trips/south-dakota/our-backyard-black-hills-national-forest/.
2. "2016 State of the Sport—U.S. Road Race Trends," *Running USA*, May 5, 2016, http://www.runningusa.org/state-of-sport-us-trends-2015.
3. Merrill C. Tenney and Moises Silva, gen. eds, *The Zondervan Encyclopedia of the Bible*, Volume 1 (Grand Rapids: Zondervan, 2009), 1106.
4. John Ortberg, speaker, Communicating Conference 2003: Anatomy of a Message, Willow Creek Community Church, October 20–21, 2003.

Chapter 17: Seeing the Invisible

1. "Descartes: I think therefore I am," *Philosophy & Philosophers*, May 1, 2017, http://www.the-philosophy.com/descartes-i-think-therefore-i-am.
2. Paul Taylor, "More than Half of Millennials Have Shared a 'Selfie,'" *Pew Research Center*, March 4, 2014, http://www.pewresearch.org/fact-tank/2014/03/04/more-than-half-of-millennials-have-shared-a-selfie/.
3. Kimberly Wang, "The Average Millennial Spends This Much Time Taking Selfies Each Week," *Brit + Co*, February 25, 2016, https://www.brit.co/millennial-selfie-study/.
4. Rachel Jacoby Zoldan, "This Is the Estimated Number of Selfies You'll Take in a Lifetime," *TeenVogue*, March 31, 2017, https://www.teenvogue.com/story/samsung-number-of-selfies-lifetime.
5. James Franco, "The Meanings of the Selfie," *The New York Times*, December 26, 2013, http://www.nytimes.com/2013/12/29/arts/the-meanings-of-the-selfie.html.
6. "Malala's Story," *Malala Fund*, https://www.malala.org/malalas-story.
7. R. J. Palacio, *Wonder* (New York: Knopf Books for Young Readers,

2012), 313.

8. Mark Glanville, "Jesus ate his way through the gospels—eaten with a tax-collector recently?" . . . *for he has made you beautiful* (blog), July 20, 2012, https://markrglanville.wordpress.com/2012/07/20/jesus-ate-his-way-through-the-gospels-eaten-with-a-tax-collector-recently/.

9. John J. Parsons, "Hebrew Names of God," *Hebrew4Christians*, http://www.hebrew4christians.com/Names_of_G-d/El/el.html.

10. *Iron Man*, directed by Jon Favreau (Paramount Pictures, Marvel Studios, 2008), DVD.

Chapter 18: Becoming a Powerful Symbol

1. "What Does the 'S' Stand for?" YouTube video, 0:15, from *Man of Steel*, posted by "Shady15," June 6, 2013, https://www.youtube.com/watch?v=aKmRt8UgMps.

2. Catherine Hezser, *Jewish Literacy in Roman Palestine*, (Tübingen, Germany: Mohr Siebeck, 2001).

3. Bart D. Ehrman, *Did Jesus Exist?: The Historical Argument for Jesus of Nazareth* (Kindle Locations 702–712). Harper Collins, Inc. Kindle Edition.

4. "What is the ICHTHUS?" The Bible Study Site, http://www.biblestudy.org/biblepic/christian-fish-symbol.html.

5. Elesha Coffman, "What Is the Origin of the Christian Fish Symbol?" Ask the Editors, *Christianity Today*, August 8, 2008, http://www.christianitytoday.com/history/2008/august/what-is-origin-of-christian-fish-symbol.html.

6. "What is the ICHTHUS?" The Bible Study Site, http://www.biblestudy.org/biblepic/christian-fish-symbol.html.

Chapter 19: Moving at the Speed of Light

1. Cari Haus, "How Far Did Jesus Walk?" https://s3.amazonaws.com/storage.nm-storage.com/calvaryslc/downloads/loc008_how_far_did_jesus_walk.pdf.

2. Frank A. Gaebelein, ed., *The Expositor's Bible Commentary: Matthew, Mark, Luke*, Volume 8 (Grand Rapids: Zondervan, 1984), 622.

3. Joe Martino, "The Top 5 Regrets of the Dying," *HUFFPOST*, August 3, 2013, http://www.huffingtonpost.com/2013/08/03/top-5-regrets-of-the-dying_n_3640593.html.

4. Craig Groeschel, *Weird: Because Normal Isn't Working* (Grand Rapids: Zondervan, 2012), 33.

Chapter 20: Your Greatest Villain

1. Anna B. Wroblewska, "How Gyms Make Money," *The Motley Fool*, May 23, 2015, http://www.fool.com/investing/general/2015/05/23/exorcise-your-ghosts-of-spending-past.aspx.

Chapter 21: The Power of Legacy
   1. Acts 4:13 KJV.

Super Discussion Questions
   1. C. S. Lewis, *The Weight of Glory* (1949; repr., New York: HarperOne, 2001), 46.

SUPER DISCUSSION QUESTIONS

▶ What superpower would you love to have? How do you imagine that ability would change your life for the better? The worse?

▶ Why do you think people today are so obsessed with superheroes?

▶ Read this quote from C. S. Lewis and discuss its meaning:

There are no *ordinary* people. You have never talked to a mere mortal. Nations, cultures, arts, civilisations—these are mortal, and their life is to ours as the life of a gnat. But it is immortals whom we joke with, work with, marry, snub, and exploit.[1]

▶ How hard is it to see yourself as extraordinary? As a believer in Christ, what makes you extraordinary? How would you treat people differently if you saw them as extraordinary?

▶ In the story of Batman, the villain Bane throws Batman into a prison to keep him from rescuing Gotham. What prisons are holding you back from making a difference in the world? Anxiety, addiction, debt, laziness, guilt, insecurity, a perceived lack of talent? What are you going to do to rise above that prison?

▶ Think of at least one person in your life who feels like an underdog. Take a moment to send them a text, email, or even a handwritten letter to encourage them.

▶ In Thomas à Kempis's book *The Imitation of Christ,* he says, "Take delight in being unknown." In a culture obsessed with celebrities and selfies, are you able to take delight in being unknown? What are some disadvantages of being famous?

▶ Why is a heart for adventure important for a hero? When is a time that God prompted you to step outside your comfort zone or called you to do something you never imagined? Are there any areas of your life that you have deemed off limits to God?

▶ In the book *Who Moved My Cheese?* Dr. Spencer Johnson asks, "What would you do if you were not afraid?" How different would your life look if fear was not an obstacle?

▶ Read Paul's words to Timothy: "For God has not given us a spirit of fear and timidity, but of power, love, and self-discipline" (2 Tim. 1:7 NLT). Now list the top three things you

fear, and ask God what you need to overcome those fears.
Read Jeremiah 29:7: "Seek the peace and prosperity of the
city. . . . Pray to the LORD for it, because if it prospers, you too
will prosper." What are some ways you can strive to protect
the city, i.e., the things that God has placed under your care?

▶ Spider-Man didn't want to use his powers to protect the
city at first, assuming it was not his responsibility. What are
some reasons people neglect protecting the things God has
placed under their care?

▶ On a scale of 1 to 10 (1 being a coach potato and 10
being the mom of a toddler), how busy have you been lately?
What are some things in your schedule that keep you from
being open to God's leading?

▶ Name someone who you think does an excellent job
managing his or her schedule. What do you think is the
secret to that person's success?

▶ What will the next generation inherit from your life and
legacy? How do you want to be remembered? What do you
need to change in order to create that kind of memory?

▶ How has Jesus' resurrection shaped not just your faith
but your life? Does Easter make a tangible difference in your
attitude and actions, or would your life be the same if Jesus
hadn't risen from the dead?

▶ Are you "foolish" enough to believe that YOU can make a difference in the world? Why or why not?

▶ Albert Einstein once said, "The world is a dangerous place to live; not because of the people who are evil, but because of the people who don't do anything about it." Pick one thing to do this week that will prove change is possible when the ordinary who love God RISE.

ACKNOWLEDGMENTS

In the world of comic books, superheroes face challenges so great they need a team to help them. In the DC Universe, it's the Justice League; and in the Marvel Universe, it's the Avengers. When it came to this book, there was a team of people willing to suit up and go all in with me.

I want to say a huge thank you to The Well Church for giving me the space and inspiration to tackle this project. A special shout out to Jason Ingram, Family Pastor, exceptional leader, and an even better friend. You make us the perfect dynamic duo.

To my agent Dan Balow—you are the Batman who connected me to a super publishing team. Thank you to Moody Publishers for believing in this book and helping me make it a reality. A super fist bump to Ingrid Beck and Amanda Cleary Eastep for making me sound like a better writer than I really am through their editorial magic.

A bonus thank you to my wife Suzanne. If I had an equivalent of the Bat-signal, it would be a giant S, because there's no one I would rather fight "crime" with than you. And to my mother and father-in-law who always go up, up and a way beyond.

Finally, thank you to the real hero, Jesus Christ, who saved my life. I could not have finished this book without Your inspiration, encouragement, strength, wisdom, and peace. Thank You for the privilege of joining Your Team.